Dear Limits,
GET OUT
OF MY WAY.

Dear Limits, GET OUT OF MY WAY.

*The Woman's Guide To End Self Limitations
And Push Past Social Restrictions*

By Ky-Lee Hanson

Contributing Authors:
Kelly Rolfe, Rusiana T Mannarino, Cindi Melkerson,
Deirdre Slattery, Elaine McMillan, Emily Marie Gruzinski,
Jennifer Jayde, Jess Arbour, Jewell Siebert,
Katherine Debs, Lisa Gartly, Sabrina Greer, Shabira Wahab,
Shelbi De Silva, Vickee Love, Angelia Mantis

Published in Canada, for Global Distribution by Golden Brick Road Publishing House Inc. www.goldenbrickroad.pub

Dear Women Book Series Girl Illustration: by Natalie Barratt

For more information email: kylee@gbrpublicationsagency.com

ISBN: trade paperback   978-1-988736-09-9
       ebook   978-1-988736-10-5

To order additional copies of this book: orders@gbrph.ca

Table of Contents

"When you grow up you tend to get told the world is the way it is and you're life is just to live your life inside the world. Try not to bash into the walls too much. Try to have a nice family, have fun, save a little money.

That's a very limited life.

Life can be much broader once you discover one simple fact: Everything around you that you call life was made up by people that were no smarter than you and you can change it, you can influence it, you can build your own things that other people can use.

Once you learn that, you'll never be the same again."
~ Steve Jobs

Preface

Dear Limits, Get Out Of My Way is a compilation book written by women primarily for women. My name is Ky-Lee Hanson and I am the lead author, visionary, and compiler of this book series. This book was created to help people recognize limitations in their world, learn how to push past them, and continue on towards their limitless potential. It is a progression from the first volume of the *Dear Women Guide Book Series*, titled, *Dear Stress, I'm Breaking Up With You.* My understanding is that a person with a clear mind is capable of more, than that of a mind polluted by stress. Our first book helps people to move out of a cluttered state of mind and get focused on what is *actually* important. From there, a person could have a clearer view of what is truly blocking them, is it a brick wall that society built or is it their own personal self judgement, or maybe it is someone in their life causing restrictions. When you have moments of stress-free clarity, you can look around constructively, identify limitations and strategically plan to move past them, and maybe, *just maybe*, find the opportunity within the limitation.

This book will help you identify limitations you may not realize you have such as fears, self limiting habits and thoughts, maybe an unhealthy or undefined relationship with a partner, friend or family member, your relationship with money or your own self judgement and "not-always-positive" self image. Any of these limitations could be blocking you from moving forward.

With this book, you are ready to take your life in a new direction. Does that mean quit your job, get a divorce, move across seas or lose 20 pounds? No, not always. Situations in our external world do not always need to change drastically for us to feel and BE limitless. Your power is inside you, maybe you just haven't seen it in a while. Maybe your boss or child dictates your day-to-day life and you simply don't have time for yourself, or so you think. Are you letting someone else limit your growth and dreams? Is your perception of time a limitation? Let's talk about time and tonality for a moment.

First, so you know, this is not a sugar-coated book. We are going to tell you straight up how *we* got from one place to the next, and we expect you to crush down a wall or two along the way. Then there is "time", ok *now* I'm getting started, there *is* plenty of time, it is simply what we choose to prioritize, not about how many hours are in the day. I know I have time for the gym, I could even watch tv, check social media or research while I am on the exercise bike - multi-task, right? *I know, I know, put down your phone - be in the moment.* Well doll, I am not a life coach, I am a momentum, get-it-done, business coach. But honestly back to my point, I just don't like the gym. I'm not going to lie to myself and say, "I don't have the time."

Tip #1 Stop lying to yourself. Tip #2 Stop limiting yourself.

Let me be clear, and perhaps you feel the same, I really do not think I have balance in my life, *but* I do get to spend my time doing what I enjoy the most; my career. It's no longer my first choice to spend my weekends socializing; I spent my childhood, teenage years and 20's doing that. It may sometimes feel as though I don't have many friends, but I spend all day really getting to know people within the business I am building, my coauthors have become very close to me, and if I want to put the time in, the most amazing people are there for me to get to know and let them know me. Unfortunately, I need to make sacrifices right now. We all do. It is not that I do not have the time, I CAN make the time; instead, I have made a choice to prioritize my business and my own personal development. Next will come self-care. Time or lack-thereof is not a limit, my busy schedule is not a limit, it is my chosen priority. Sacrifice does not have to mean elimination, maybe instead, it is an internal compromise and strategic allocation of time also known as a choice. Here is what I do, I make friends within my career and interests, I involve my friends in my work, and I involve my friends in physical activity - no gym - but dance classes, swimming and sauna. Recently, I decided that I wasn't going to limit myself anymore from physical activity, self care, and friendships because my career is *more important* and my preferences differ from popular pastimes such as the gym and weekend socializing aka nightclubs. There is always a way to work towards balance or at least, compromise. We just need to think outside the box. Remember, that box is a limit! I recently watched the movie, *Minimalism*. Here is an explanation from their website, *"What is minimalism? If we had to sum it up in a single sentence, we would say, Minimalism is a tool to rid yourself of life's excess in favor of focusing on what's important—so you can find happiness, fulfillment, and freedom."* [1] In the movie, they also explain my point of view on friendships and time allocation as something along the lines of, we should only spend time and be in the company of people with the same interests as us. Otherwise, the relationship is wasteful. We are being wasteful of our time within the wrong environments. Life is not for wasting, it is for living - it is not fair to anyone when you wrongfully allocate time. Minimalism and being conscious does not mean to cut off all ties with people, to never indulge, throw away all your belongings or that you can never shop again - *my goodness, I would never survive that!* I DO have a minimalist outlook on where and how I spend my time, and I feel this decision and way of life prevents many obstacles and limitations. It has not yet illuminated over to my wardrobe, possessions, or papers - *why are there always so many pieces of paper everywhere!* - but, I do focus on what is important to me first and foremost. I do not like to waste time, energy, and emotions on what does not serve me. I will be quick to make choices as I know myself, and these choices do not always favor others. I do not limit myself around making other people happy or living up to their expectations. *I am Miss. Anti-Expectations!* If what I do makes me happy, is constructive and benefits the consensus, the right people will come to visit my world. Similarly, I expect the people in my life to put themselves first also; one of few "expectations" that I do side with. Expectations is a hot topic in this book series. Many people by nature are typically unrealistic with their expectations. Some have a *right now* or *all or nothing* mentality, and tend to put unrealistic deadlines on goals, and in turn, create blocks and limit their growth period. There is a check out date if things do not meet

---

[1]Millburns, J. F., Nicodemus, R (n.d) *What is Minimalism?* Retrieved from http://www.theminimalists.com/minimalism/

up to the maximum ideal. When people think like this - If I am not married in 3 years, I am out, as the clock is ticking, or if my business does not profit in 6 months, I will go back to work - the mind has a back door and one foot already out. If you are not all in, and cannot see the value in what you will experience, then this is an expectation likely programmed from social-norms *and* you have self inflicted it as a limitation. The check-out date is a pre-determined, pressured exit and limits the goal from developing.

Do not worry. We have all been there, and will always be working to reprogram and crush limitations in various aspects of our life. That is what we are here to share with you.

Up and onwards to the limitless you!

Truly,

Ky-Lee Hanson

Founder and Lead Author

kylee@gbrpublicationsagency.com

Introduction

By Ky-Lee Hanson and Tania J Moraes-Vaz

"Taking jobs to build up your resume,
is the same as saving up sex for old age." ~ Warren Buffett

Limitations are disguised in the form of experiences, environments, people, expectations, social-norms, stereotypes and of course our own personal truths, beliefs, and reality. They are often markers that show us what needs to change, and where we need to reassess these various forms of limitations.

As time evolves, so do we. We are not the same person today, that we were last year, last month, or even a few hours ago. There are events and shifts that occur in our life that serve to change us, and propel us to seek growth for ourselves - a life of purpose, a life of quality, a life filled with constant growth. What is growth? In this book, we relate growth mostly to personal development. Personal development is an internal exploration, learning, and adoption of spirituality, the human condition, inner strength, self esteem, self confidence, as well as, communication (which includes listening) skills and stress management. This journey develops you into a self aware human being. A self aware, strong, and confident person will then be able to grow and flex within social development and career development. Furthermore, with growth comes the shedding of that which no longer serves us, our purpose, or goals in life - essentially, a call to move beyond these limitations. This can include doing away with old patterns, habits, thoughts or behaviors; but moreover, this will involve letting go and moving on from the individuals who are not a positive influence in your life, and no longer add any value to it as a result. As Jim Rohn says, *"You are the average of the five people you spend the most time with."* As such, we often underestimate the extent to which our habits, patterns, and our outlook on life is influenced by those we associate with the most - positive or negative, and also by our own thoughts which can sometimes be limiting, or negative. It will seem hard at first, scary as well, but take my word for it, the best thing you can do for yourself is to cut out those who drain you, do not bring out the best in you, and who are not genuinely happy for you. Instead, surround yourself with people who inspire you, elevate the quality of your life and lift you higher. This can have a powerful impact in your life - personally, as well as professionally. This transcends into your own self talk, the activities you partake in, the companies and organizations you support, the education you study, the job you do and also, the way *you* treat people.

We will examine and learn how to push past one's internal and external limitations by choosing to live a life brimming with motivation and momentum; a life where we rise up beyond our own personal limitations as well as the limitations placed upon us by our sociocultural environment, and our relationships. Equally important to this is identifying the relationship we have with ourselves, and with others around us. Feeling limited, and perceiving yourself as stuck in a particular relationship, or environment can be detrimental and have unpleasant effects on one's emotional and mental being in the long run. What is worse is that we may not even be aware that the way we perceive ourselves is limiting us, or that a relationship, situation, or an environment is unhealthy for us, thus hindering our growth and progress.

They say energy is contagious; be it positive or negative, it doesn't matter. Therefore, you really need to examine the quality of people you surround yourself with, and the environments you live within. Are they a positive or negative influence? Will they help you thrive, or hold you back? This is one of the first steps in surpassing your personal limitations. Since internal limitations stem from external influences, it is imperative that we examine those influences, and see how they add or detract value from our lives, our aspirations and goals, and hence our world. In turn, we may also start becoming aware of how we ourselves may be adding to our limitations through our habits, thought processes, or behaviors that may actually be limiting us, instead of propelling us forward.

This book is a call to exceed your own personal expectations, and rise above whatever you believe is limiting you from living the life that you want. Visually, limitations are like a set of stepping stones in the stream of life. We cannot leap forward, unless we are willing to leave the past behind. We cannot pursue the greatness that we are personally destined for, unless we are willing to take risks - take that leap of faith in the opportunities that we come across. Moreover, we cannot live a fulfilled life without taking a giant leap of faith in ourselves - our abilities, and the talents we each have to offer.

"Don't let time be a limit.
Don't let 'good enough' be a limit.
Don't let lack of experien ce be a limit.
Instead, make these your opportunities."
~ Ky-Lee Hanson

Section 1

Great Expectations Will Not Limit Me

Featuring

Jewell Siebert, Sabrina Greer, Deirdre Slattery, Shelbi De Silva,
and Shabira Wahab

Opening commentary by Tania J Moraes-Vaz

As women, we most often limit ourselves emotionally, and mentally, which then flows into other facets of our daily life. This affects the choices and decisions we make on a day to day basis. We end up doing this often by either taking on a *Yes sir, Yes Ma'am* attitude - where we are afraid to say no to a person, a situation, or an environment that does not help us grow and evolve positively, or we let the external opinions and doubts of those around us seep into our consciousness. We then allow these factors to limit our thinking and perspective, and play into the great expectations expected of us by those around us.

How we feel about ourselves on a physical, mental and emotional level has directly affects our relationship with others. Consider this, if we had to toss aside all of the preconceived notions of how we, as women, are supposed to look, think, feel, act, and be with ourselves and with others - How would you choose to see yourself? What are the words and catchphrases that come to mind when you think of describing yourself - your very essence, your body image, your persona? How do these words and catchphrases make you feel? What would you choose to wear? How would you choose to show up for yourself, your environment, job / business and in your relationships? Do these words and thoughts elicit a happy, confident, and radiant response, or does it make you feel anxious, doubtful, and not so good about yourself?

Some food for thought: Did you know that models were originally chosen thin in terms of their physique, to reflect how clothes hang in their original form, as art? Thin was as close as it got to visualizing the way an outfit would hang, as it would on a hanger; Moreover, it was a way for the designer to see if the outfit looked how they envisioned it. It was people who began to compare themselves to models - unfortunately over time, people's lack of self confidence and their constant need to compare themselves to one another, spurred on a huge financial opportunity for the beauty, fashion, diet, health and wellness therapy industries. Nobody truly thought to examine the rationale and history behind why thin was a criteria in the selection of fashion models. Model selection was simply a way to display clothing; couture as art, in as much of its original form as possible. It was never a statement on how one should look like, or even aspire to do so.[2]

Recently, there was a splendid and powerful performance given by Lady Gaga at the 2017 Super Bowl - it was amazing to see such a huge social icon deliver an empowering performance focused solely on her music and creativity. However, the very next day, an article circulating online on MensHealth.com[3] was discussing how people were body shaming her for an instance where her midriff was showing during her performance; conversely, majority of the internet fan following came right to her defense and shut down the body shamers. Additionally, the individual who originally shared this article on Facebook commented that she knew the moment Lady Gaga took off her jacket, the internet would call her fat. This just goes to show how conditioned we are, especially as women, to view ourselves and each other based on the ideals set for us by the socio-cultural environment we have been living in. This in turn adds to the myriad of self esteem and body image issues that constantly plague our daily lives, both personally and professionally. We need to reprogram our subconscious to initially go to a place of acceptance, not a place of judgment ... we encourage social expectations. Hence, self love and the way we view and feel about ourselves is a huge movement today. It is a movement to un-condition and un-learn decades of programmed subconscious thinking of "not being enough - not beautiful enough, not strong enough, not feminine enough," based on the perceptions and ideals placed upon us by ourselves and the society we live in. These consciously subconscious ideals often affect us on a bigger scale than we like to admit. It affects our relationship with ourselves and with others, the professions we may choose to pursue or not pursue, the opportunities we may either seize or let pass us by.

In our first section, discover how to assert self-love, establish boundaries, and reclaim your power while nurturing your inner goddess by learning how to break these barriers and achieve a healthy outlook

---

[2] Clements, K. (2013, July 05). *Former Vogue editor: The truth about size zero.* Retrieved from https://www.theguardian.com/fashion/2013/jul/05/vogue-truth-size-zero-kirstie-clements

[3] Hrustic, A (2016, February 07). *People Can't Stop Talking About Lady Gaga's "Belly" and the Internet Is Not Having It.* Retrieved from http://www.menshealth.com/weight-loss/lady-gaga-body-shaming

on your current self and the reality that you are experiencing. Jewell calls us to explore, examine, and unlearn how to push past the limitations of these ideals, and truly learn to embrace ourselves for who we are; to know and realize that we are enough; to let that knowledge itself carry you through your personal and professional endeavours, and to never let anyone else define who you are, or what you are capable of accomplishing. Next, Sabrina shows us how to how to juggle and balance the chaotic lifestyles we lead by finding beauty and peace amidst chaos, while learning to identify when we have veered off center and balance. She shows us how to come back to it from a place of gratitude, rest, and relaxation. She shows us that balance isn't always what we ideally consider it to be, and nor will it look the same as anyone else's; rather balance is subjective, and is as much a state of mind and perspective. Deirdre encourages us to learn how to start being comfortable in the very own essence of who we are, by reframing and rebuilding our view of body image into a positive one by envisioning, showing up, and dressing up for success, while owning the success that comes our way. Learn to embrace your personal style with Shelbi, and make a fashion statement based on comfort, yet enough of that oomph factor to make you feel good, and conquer whatever life throws your way. Remember, the outfit doesn't wear you, rather, you wear the outfit. Lastly, Shabira guides us on how to gain an awareness of the way we show up in our various relationships, and learn how to establish boundaries, and meet our relationships halfway.

Chapter 1

Sticks And Stones

by Jewell Siebert

"The eyes of others our prisons; their thoughts our cages."
~ Virginia Woolf

Jewell Siebert

After 42 hours of labor, the nurse handed Jewell her tiny, pink, perfect little baby, and in that moment she knew. She thought, "I work too much, I'm miserable and stressed out, and I need to make a change. Every decision I make will have a ripple effect on this perfect little human, and I'm going to create a life I love for both of us."

Seven days later, after 14 years of service and multiple trips to Iraq and Afghanistan, Jewell submitted her resignation from the army. Six months later, she left active duty for the Army Reserves, and began the next chapter in her life.

Today, Jewell Siebert is a #1 international bestselling author, intuitive coach, and Certified Canfield Trainer in *The Success Principles*. She supports working women to actually enjoy the lives they work so hard to create. She uses her real world experience and unique perspective to help her clients make more time for the things they love, overcome blocks that keep them living small, and find true joy in their lives.

She lives in Austin, Texas with her husband and daughter, where she takes full advantage of the city's BBQ scene.

support@jewellsiebert.com | www.jewellsiebert.com
ig: jewell.siebert | fb: jewellsiebertcoach | t: jewell_siebert

I could feel my cheeks burning. My throat tightened up. The sinking feeling of inadequacy filled my stomach. Everyone was looking at me, turned around in their seats, witnessing my humiliation. It was my senior year of high school, and word had gotten around that I was going to college at the United States Military Academy at West Point. Mr. S was subbing for physics that day, and was taking the opportunity to tell me that I wouldn't make it through my first summer at West Point. Didn't I know that it's tough there? That people yell at you? That they do push-ups? Someone snickered. I had never wished to get back to Sir Isaac's theories so badly in my life. Yes, I realized it was a semi-crazy choice for me. I had never planned on joining the military, I *was* a soft-spoken and gentle person, and honestly, I wasn't sure if I would make it. But still…I didn't expect to be discouraged by my teacher in public. Mr. S wasn't the only person with misgivings. Up until graduation, my school counselor and some of the other teachers repeatedly told my mom and I that I couldn't go to West Point, and that I wouldn't be able to make it through the initial summer training. Now, I loved my teachers and knew they were truly concerned for my wellbeing and were trying to trying to keep me from making what they thought was a terrible mistake; it was disheartening to have so many people tell me I was going to fail. That was the first time people had expressed negative opinions about my career in the military, but it certainly wasn't the last. Believe it or not, some people think that women don't belong in the military (groundbreaking news, I know). It always surprised me - and stung a little more - when another *woman* was the one sharing that sentiment. The next time that happened, I was an awkward freshman - called a "Plebe." I had short hair, big clunky brown glasses, and I looked more like the scrawny before version of Captain America than the latter. I was easily flustered by the constant yelling of the upperclassmen who made developing me their special project. I wasn't the best at memorizing knowledge, the required information all cadets are supposed to learn, and often found myself standing at attention, stammering out gibberish, and wishing for time to pass by quicker. But on that day, I couldn't have been happier. The West Point Parents Club of Michigan was visiting and throwing their annual tailgate party, and I got to spend the weekend with my mom. After the football tailgate ended, my mom crammed her Oldsmobile Cutlass Ciera full of cadets and their friends, and drove them back to the barracks area. One of the people, a classmate's visiting civilian girlfriend, started talking about how she didn't think women should be allowed at West Point, or in the military at all. I sat there dumbfounded that A) a woman in the 20th century was saying those words, and B) that a woman in the 20th century was saying those words *while sitting in the backseat of my mother's car.* I don't remember how the conversation ended, but it definitely did not end with me retorting with a snappy comeback about how she must just bawl into her apron every time she thinks about us women who are stepping out of our "rightful place." What I do remember was my burning cheeks, the knot in my throat, and that same sinking feeling in my stomach, reminding me that *maybe I wasn't good enough* and that *I didn't belong there.*

Frankly, Scarlet....

There was nothing unique about this situation. All of us have dealt with others' limiting beliefs at some point in our lives. To a certain degree, we all have ingrained opinions on how people should act, and what roles everyone plays. We all have certain biases and expectations, whether flattering or not, that affect how we see ourselves and others. Oftentimes, they are based on how you look, what you wear, or as I experienced with my teachers and the girlfriend, your personality and which chromosomes you drew in the DNA lottery. These things create our label, and it can be incredibly powerful. The labels people give us can either empower us or limit us, depending on how we receive and process the information. There are two main ways others' beliefs can limit us: by putting up external barriers (such as barring from employment, clubs, or social circles), or by fuelling self-limiting beliefs inside our own minds. The first one is often outside our control, and not a topic for this chapter. It is the latter of these issues - how external labels and expectations affect our inner dialog - that is much more powerful, and what I believe our time is best spent on overcoming.

Negative things that others believe and say can only affect us if there is already a nugget of doubt existing in our minds. Think of something you are really proud of in your life. For example, you volunteer at a food bank on weekends to help the less fortunate. If someone came up as you were stocking the pantry and called you selfish, would you believe them? Of course not! You would think they had a screw loose, or were having a bad day, or just didn't know the first thing about you. Their opinion of you wouldn't affect how you saw yourself. However, if you're already doubting something about yourself, that negative input from an external source acts like kindling for self-limiting beliefs. If you, like I was in my Plebe year, are questioning your abilities and your worth in an area, and someone else shares their negative opinions with you, it will solidify that doubt within your mind. The little voice inside your head will latch onto that feedback, and replay it over and over, reminding you to play small, keeping you stuck.

It's Not Me, It's You

The good news is that you have a choice. External opinions and biases can limit, but they can also empower. Surely, one could accept external labels and limitations as truth, and decide to act within the confines of that paradigm, or one could decide that others' labels and expectations are simply their opinions, not fact. Once you recognize that the things people say are merely reflections of their own limiting beliefs, based on their own fears and biases, it becomes much easier to disown them. Now, here's where it gets really good: **when you don't own someone's judgements of your abilities as your own, you're free to look for the learning point inside the message. You can use their negative input to fuel your own success.** Now, you may be thinking, "What the heck are you talking about? So when someone expresses a negative opinion about my abilities, I not only have to just shrug it off, but I also have to dissect it for things that I could use? How the heck am I supposed to do that, when all I want to do is wring their little judgmental necks??" Or something to that effect... Yes, I fully acknowledge that remaining emotionally detached from naysayers' opinions can be difficult to do, but it does provide you with a healthy way of dealing with negative feedback, AND it does get easier with time and practice. Plus, I have several tips and tricks to help you do it.

Empowerment Strategies

The secret to making others limiting beliefs work for you is to strengthen your mindset and belief in your own greatness. Then, you can reframe them and choose whether or not to accept them as a tool for your growth and success. For the record, I chose not to accept the beliefs of the people who didn't think I belonged at West Point. Not only did I make it through my first summer, but I graduated, spent 14 years on active duty, and am currently a Lieutenant Colonel in the Army Reserves. So, yes - totally doable.

Here are some methods I like to use:

Assess Your Strengths And Weaknesses, And Create A Plan To Develop The Areas You'd Like To Improve

In order to be able to assess the validity of others' expressed opinions, it is helpful to really know yourself. One of the best ways to get an accurate picture of who you are, and to improve your chances of future success, is to do a self-assessment.

This can be as easy as writing a list of your strengths and weaknesses, but I encourage you to take it a step further. Ask your friends and families for input - for both the wonderful and the not so great. I'm not going to pretend like this is an easy task. It's hard to ask for constructive criticism from those you love. In the army, we have to do a survey every few years, where we ask for anonymous feedback from our peers, subordinates, and superiors. I literally sweat every time I hit the send button on that thing. No one likes hearing how they're not measuring up. But, to quote G.I. Joe, *"Knowing is half the battle."* Once you know those areas in which you could use a little improvement, you can create a plan to improve that area, and as a result, be more confident in your abilities (not to mention more successful). Plus, I guarantee you that you'll also get all kinds of amazing, make-you-teary compliments about how great you are. The simplest way to do this is to send an email or text message asking for the feedback. Or if you'd like to do this anonymously, you could create a free survey online in just a few minutes. By understanding your strengths and weaknesses, you are better equipped to handle others' criticism. This way, even if others do comment on one of your weaknesses, you'll be less affected, as you already know it's an issue, and you've developed a plan to strengthen that aspect of yourself.

Seek Internal Validation

External validation is great. It feels amazing to be appreciated. That's why gold stars are such an effective reward for school kids. We never outgrow that love of being appreciated for our talents. However, if we exclusively pursue validation, we become more vulnerable to external (limiting) beliefs, and more likely to develop habits such as people-pleasing. Rather, we can develop our sense of personal pride, and focus on seeking internal validation. One great way to do this is to practice the mirror exercise. Before bed, I like to give myself an *attagirl*. I make eye contact with myself in the mirror (this feels a little funny at first, but is a critical component), and say, "Jewell, you did so great today." Then I list out the wins I had, the temptations I overcame, the times I was nice, and the things for which I'm grateful. Then I close by saying "I love you," and hold eye contact for a minute to soak it all in. Will this feel strange? Probably. Will your family members tease you about it? Maybe. But who cares? It works. Now, the most important thing about this exercise is that no negative self-talk is allowed. If the little voice inside your head starts bringing up things you did not do or hints that your accomplishments aren't that noteworthy, you shut it down. Thank the voice for it's input, tell it - *not useful*, and get back to focusing on the good stuff. This one exercise will have profound effects on your mindset, and will steel you against others' limiting beliefs. Try it for a week, and *then* let me know how your life has improved.

Remind Yourself Of Past Successes

It can be easy to focus on the negative. You could get 10 compliments on a report you wrote, but the one thing that will linger in your mind is the one critical comment. That's just how we're wired. It's part of the reason why our species has survived (along with the development of delicious java drinks, of course). But, it doesn't serve us to focus solely on the negative. Reminding ourselves of past wins helps to fuel our self-worth, keep our energy levels high, and rise above negative input from those who would otherwise limit us. A great way to do this is to keep a *win* journal. Whenever you accomplish something great - whether big or small - write it in your journal. Then, go back and review what you wrote on a regular basis. Not only does this feel wonderful, but it also gives you a fantastic resource to disprove the negative comments from others.

Question, Question, Question

Oftentimes, others' limiting beliefs are based on a bias or worldview that simply isn't true. However, sometimes these false truths are so ingrained in our society that they are difficult to recognize as opinions, and not fact. Vishen Lakhiani, CEO of Mindvalley, beautifully explains this phenomenon is his talk on *brules*, or B.S. rules. When someone expresses her limiting belief to you, ask yourself if that's true. Really question it. Ask yourself, "What would happen / what would life be like if the opposite was true?" You may be pleasantly surprised with the answer - that what you *knew* to be an undeniable fact was actually just a *brule* posing as truth.

Play The "How Does This Serve Me?" Game

Here's the part where we flip the script and use the external opinions to our advantage. Instead of getting defensive about of the person's limiting beliefs, ask yourself, "What can I learn from this? What is the universe teaching me? What is my opportunity?" Just by reframing the input as a *lesson with a positive intent* removes a lot of the emotional charge from the situation. Now, you might need to distance yourself from the person, and take a few deep breaths before you're ready to implement this step, but it's definitely worth doing. I believe that every setback, every challenge, heck, every annoying driver who cuts us off on the expressway can teach us something, if *we* let them. If we seize this opportunity as a gift rather than a hurtful piece of information, we can grow and achieve so much more in our lives. It's kind of a twist on the saying, *"Don't get mad, get even."* Well, without the vindictive undertone... I'm not condoning any kind of Michael Corleone stuff here. For example, when I was applying to West Point, several teachers and the school counselor told me that I wouldn't make it there - that I was too skinny, too quiet and too gentle to survive military life. It stung for sure, but I took their words, and used them as fuel when I felt like giving up. Don't get upset by what someone thinks you can't do - get out there and prove them wrong!

It's Your Choice

Being on the receiving end of others' limiting beliefs is inevitable. How many times do our family members offer us well-meaning advice on what we should, or shouldn't be doing with our lives? But the choice of what we do with that information is absolutely our choice. How we accept or reject the truth of those limiting beliefs has the potential to impact not only our sense of self-worth, but also our ability to make the kind of impact that we want to have in the world. By strengthening our mindset, and asking key questions, we can turn those limiting beliefs into a force of good in our lives. I know my choice. What's yours?

Chapter 2

Balancing Buckets

by Sabrina Greer

"Life is like riding a bicycle. To keep balance, you must keep moving."
~ Albert Einstein

Sabrina Greer

Entrepreneur | Model | Blogger | Supermom | World Traveller |
Aspiring Philanthropist | Student of the Universe

Sabrina Greer knew from a young age that her life's purpose was to fulfil her 3 passions: Save the world (philanthropy), see the world (travel) and shape the world (working with the young minds of the future). It sounds like a tall order, but not for this lady. Sabrina's passion for life, and stubborn drive to succeed are impenetrable.

Her journey started when she was a child, and her parents decided to become foster parents for predominantly special needs children. She learned compassion, empathy, and a strong desire to help others. At the ripe age of 15, the next milestone began when she was offered her first international modelling contract. Not one to ever pass up an adventure, this brave, young, free spirit embarked on what became a 10+ year career as an internationally recognized model, actor and spokesperson with contracts like *Sports Illustrated* and *Harper's Bazaar* magazine.

After 10 years of globetrotting, she found home base back in Ontario, Canada (her origin), and decided to earn her degree in education and developmental psychology alongside working 3 jobs. Post education, she dabbled in the corporate world as an events director, quickly realizing that her superpowers lay in entrepreneurialism and helping others discover their potential through sharing opportunity and inspirational writing. Now, a wife to the man of her dreams and mother to 3 incredible boys, she spends her days being present and "working" out of her lakefront cottage office!

www.momofboys.me | www.sabrinagreer.arbonne.ca
ig: sabbygreer | mom.of.boys.3 fb: sabbygreer | momofprinces

Creating Balance In The Midst Of Chaos

We all have a bucket list, you know the chicken-scratch jot notes in the back of your journal that lists all of the places you dream of seeing; vacations you yearn to take; fears that you will someday face and overcome if the world should come to an abrupt end or you are told you only have twenty-four hours to live? What if I were to tell you this list could be a reality, and it doesn't take impending doom or the apocalypse for that to be so. Yes, I know what you are likely thinking, *But what about my job?* Or, *ha, right I will just drag my three kids to South Africa to cage dive with great white sharks, or, jump out of an airplane with my bad knee.* I am sure already that in the time it has taken you to read this short paragraph, a million *reasons* as to *why* this is not *possible* or *realistic* have crossed your mind. Perhaps to name a few, no time, no money, too much to do, or my personal favorite **that just isn't possible for me**. I promise these are self-limiting beliefs and these reasons are *excuses*. I was this way once too. I was the girl with photos of sexy celebs on my wall, wishing I could be a supermodel. My other wall plastered with magazine cut outs of tropical locations from around the globe. Had I not surrendered to the universe and let it guide my path, had I let fear rule me, I may have stayed where I was; stuck and bored, living in the **reality box** society had placed on me. I was young, living in a boring small town, where the norm was to be knocked up by your farmer husband straight out of high school. I chose to rip that box open and take whatever came my way; I chose to play big, and not succumb to being small, to playing it safe. I am not a special case, this kind of life by design (or balance) is possible for anyone, and happens to be nothing but a **choice**. It all starts with defining the imbalances and realizing that all things are temporary.

Defining Imbalance - Knowing When Your Scale Is Off Kilter

Have you ever felt like you were standing in an auditorium; feet rooted; surrounded by bustling crowds; screaming at the top of your lungs, I mean until your throat and ears bleed screaming; yet, nobody can see you or hear you? How about this one, have you ever felt like you were floating in the ocean; no land in sight; no one around to save you; yet, you cannot move, scream, or swim; you are completely paralyzed? These are both examples of emotional internal drowning, something most of us experience in times of overwhelming stress and anxiety. Times where our internal balance is off kilter.

Remember that day when the kids were screaming, and punching each other after a night of no sleep. You locked your keys in the car, ended up late for work, grabbed the wrong files, dropped your brand new phone in the toilet resulting in losing all of your photos, couldn't find parking, ran out of gas, etc., (the list of completely meaningless mishaps continues)? Balance off kilter.

The dictionary defines balance as an equal distribution of weight enabling someone or something to remain upright, and the ability to move, or stay in a position without losing control or falling. These statements are absolutely relevant when applied to internal balance as well. Typically, our idea of balance is a picture of the infamous pendulum scale weighing inanimate objects, but it is important to realize that we all have an internal scale as well. This chapter will give some insight on creating this balance in a seemingly imbalanced world, something that we all crave and desire yet massively struggle to attain daily (cue harp music and a ray of light from Captain Obvious). We need an equal distribution of weight - love, passion, patience, excitement, peace, calm and quiet. We also need to discover a way to move around our daily emotions, work, family, school, relationships, needs, wants, and dreams without losing control or falling. Is this type of blissful balance achievable in reality? Well, the answer is yes, or I likely wouldn't be writing this chapter. Not only is it possible, but it is completely up to you, and within your personal control, it is all about mindset; a positive mindset of love and gratitude specifically.

So you are probably wondering what gives me the right to speak so professionally about balance, curious perhaps about my credentials? You have every right to question, especially if you were a fly on the wall in my present day to day. Currently, I am nursing a screaming newborn, while an insanely jealous toddler is yelling in my face, "Mom, don't do that," and my old soul of a ten-year-old is asking for what I call his **picky snacks** (you know, separate, beige colored meals prepared just for him). I just told my business partner I had to call her back because I could not hear her over the noise, and I am typing this at the same time, so… I honestly would not change a thing, or trade this madness for anything. I love my chaos and feel completely zen (balanced) in these moments.

So let me explain, to call me an expert on the topic of life balance would actually be a modesty statement because the definition of an **expert** is someone encompassing a special skill for a certain topic based on **knowledge** or **experience**. While I do have a degree in developmental psychology, what actually deems me an expert is the vast range of experience I have had on this topic, most of which looked like failing miserably before coming out on top. I have been that drowning girl far too many times, but now I have the privilege of sharing my learnings with the world. To know how I arrived at my expert status and found these miraculous nuggets of knowledge, it is important to understand the journey that brought me here, AKA the **experience** that imparted this wisdom. I did not have a brutal childhood, in fact, it was a rather blessed one. I find too often that people assume knowledge and experience directly correlate with negativity or trauma. It wasn't until the ripe age of fifteen when I left home, that my upside down obstacle course of failures led me to start discovering and uncovering the keys to balance. I was never abused or denied anything I wanted, my parents have been married for over forty years with barely an argument, and I was blessed with a presentable reflection in the mirror paired with a desirable body mass. My folks are currently both still with us and are retired foster parents who granted me close to one hundred siblings growing up, and recognized saints as role models. I was always popular, never bullied; I had a quick wit, decent grades, and rarely got ill. I'm not telling you this to brag or be obnoxious, but merely to explain that it is not in fact trauma or a traumatic childhood that is always the culprit in building character. Certainly, at some stage, we all turn into crazy teenagers and are set loose on the journey to self-discovery. Sometimes, the universe chooses us to impart knowledge on, and to do so we must experience the rollercoaster; this is where we truly earn our credentials. I always believed there was a greater force pulling me, guiding me, and lighting my path. My faith has always been much stronger than my fear.

I recall being fifteen and going about my fifteen-year-old business. You know life altering boy drama, raging pubescent hormones and peer-pressures to be **cool**. I so clearly remember receiving the phone call from my (what I thought at the time) silly little modeling agency that some major clients in Taiwan were interested in using my face for their campaigns. I also remember looking in the mirror thinking **this was not possible; they must have the wrong girl**. Like most fifteen-year-old girls at that time in my life the mirror was merely a tool used to view and remove food from teeth and to apply mascara generously, nothing more, certainly not a warship apparatus. Self-confidence was not a strong suit of mine at this time. So I chuckled and thought, "What the hell, what is the worst that could happen, so what if they laugh at me?" and I agreed to meet with these foreigners! You see, my entire life I was considered a daredevil, up for anything kind of gal. I saw it as **never passing up an opportunity to grow**, although some would beg to differ I received any true growth from eating a June Bug on a dare as a kid. I digress. Weeks later, I found myself in the agency's downtown Toronto office signing paperwork to depart on an airplane to Taipei for six weeks, leaving the following week. This entire experience was even more surreal than it sounds.

It must be understood that I grew up in the suburbs of Toronto, and at eleven years old moved to a town that would fit inside the high school I would have attended. That's right, town population 1300 people. My small town high school had 500 students, and everyone knew everything about everyone else. A local farm producing a pumpkin weighing over 200 pounds was riveting, front page news and nobody in my family had ever stepped foot outside of Ontario.

So, as I loaded my bags onto the luggage conveyor at Pearson International Airport a week later, and said goodbye to my entourage, in my heart, I knew I was no longer that small town girl with nothing but magazine clippings on her wall of exotic places. I would be forever changed, and different. I would now become a clipping! *I had manifested my future purely through a desire to live bigger.*

Discovering The Turning Point & Your Inner Peace

Discovering and creating inner balance requires a few skills, these are skills that can be learned and developed. The first is confidence; you need to be madly in love with yourself so you can trust yourself to make decisions, and breathe through the drama. This is the most difficult of all the skills to master. Those who saw me grace the pages of *Harper's Bazaar* magazine wearing Chanel suits or *Sports Illustrated* wearing much less, would have never assumed confidence was a struggle for me. They would see a beautiful young woman with the entire world at her disposal. Her thick blonde wavy hair insinuates she has it all; no fear, no pain. Her washboard (photoshopped) abs and tight curves naturally indicate she is loved, romanced, and free. The strength in her expression means she is never lonely, worried, or sad. I can tell you right now this was an absolute facade. These photos were merely a surface representation, or my **Insta** self (this was long before Instagram and Facebook existed) otherwise known as the pretend me. Even though I am a couple of decades older now and have a few children to add to my hips and waistline, I would rather look at me now than that fraud. It took a lot of self-beating and deprecation to realize I am awesome; the real me is awesome! Over the years I've traveled the world, lived in nearly 10 countries and traveled to over 20. I lived through Taiwan's largest earthquake and a stomach parasite in Japan. I jumped out of an airplane; climbed Machu Picchu in Peru; partied with celebrities in Hollywood, and went to raves in Germany. I lived on private charter yachts in Spain, Italy, and France; went cage diving with great white sharks in South Africa; flew a plane in Mauritius, and lived in a hut in a Zimbabwean village. I called a beach house with a private elevator my home, and also in the slums with bedbug infestations. I am an international model, a business owner, a writer, a wife, and a mother, just to name a few of the things I have experienced and crossed off my bucket list. Through all this though, one of my most vivid memories is the moment I realized **it was all up to me and that everything in this life is a choice**. I was looking at the freezing shark infested water standing on the point where the two oceans meet on a remote beach in Cape Town, South Africa. Alone as I so often was, head full of mind numbing narcotics (don't judge me, I was 20) at 4 am wondering, *What would happen if I were to just lay face up in the freezing abyss? Would God save me? Is God real? Would the Universe take me? Would I die of hypothermia? Be reincarnated? Would I be remembered, missed, become a legend or just shark food or would I infinitely disappear? What was my intention, how did I even get here?* These are the defining moments where the lowest of lows make you look deep within yourself, and find that turning point. Truthfully, at that moment I thought of jumping in and ending it all. I was a happy girl, but something was still missing. How could I even consider ending my life? I still to this day have no idea whether I was tripping out on the drugs, maybe it was my guardian angel or this so called 'higher being", or perhaps the Universe stepping in, but everything flashed before my eyes. I saw my entire life in less than a minute. Memories of my amazing childhood, all of the influences and influencers that helped shape me, and a glimpse of the future I had yet to live. It is these moments where we need to pull up our big girl pants and realize the only real way out is to save ourselves and put some weight on the other side of the scale. Take all the self-limiting beliefs, loathing, fear, pain, artificial numbing and embrace it for all of its glory; snap out of it, realize feelings are temporary, everything is temporary (even tattoos aren't permanent) and take a good hard look at the magic that surrounds us. Every single thing around us is an earth shattering miracle. The smell of the salt water, the orange fireball peeking over the flat rock of Table Mountain, the sound of the waves hitting the pristine white sand, and the very breath that filled my chest; all incredible miracles. You are a miracle, humans tend to be selfish miracles, but miracles nonetheless. It was not my time. I was being shoved with both hands, aggressively away from the darkness, life was really just beginning. *Remember, you are you because this world needs you, your lessons, your wisdom, your love, your unborn children and your experiences.*

With Love & Gratitude, Balance & Happiness Will Prevail

So, through all I have experienced and learned, my biggest takeaway is that happiness and balance already lie within you, and to fully tap into it, you must first find love and gratitude through confidence.

Love for yourself and gratitude for all of the miracles we are blessed to be surrounded by. These miracles include air; trees; clouds; water and other humans, just to name a few. There were times even while writing this chapter, where I questioned my worth and validity, **am I still a fraud?** I looked around my world at what anyone would see as pure chaos and said, **can I really be the expert on balance?** I have baby vomit in my hair; I can see my toddler smearing feces on the furniture. I am completely deprived of sleep, still have a spare tire from my empty womb, dark bags under my eyes, dark roots in my hair, and clothing that one would question if I had a home. I questioned the timing, and even backing out of writing this at one point. Then, I realized I am happy and healthy; my kids are healthy. I am in love with my life, and myself. And at the end of the day, it is ok to take a break, ask for help, slow down, and even break down, as long as you are in love and grateful, you will find balance. Finding peace in chaos, happiness in turmoil and light in darkness; it is all mindset, perspective, and finding what counterbalances. Have faith that the universe has your back, and it will, but know it's ok because **you** have your own back too.

Chapter 3

Learning To Love Yourself

by Deirdre Slattery

"If I'd known the freedom of letting go, I would never held on."
~ Rachel Firmin

Deirdre Slattery

Deirdre Slattery is a single mother of a beautiful daughter who has brought Deirdre's passion for being a healthy, positive, and strong independent woman to a new level. Deirdre is an eternal optimist, with a grounded and practical balance for how life can be. Seeing the best in people and their potential has come naturally, and one lesson that has been hard to learn is that change comes from within. No matter the lesson, it will reveal itself when the person is ready.

This free spirit has spent time travelling the globe learning about life and especially feels at home near water, surrounded by people who are thriving and living their life healthy and happily. Her love for learning about others, health and business, lead her to pursue a second career in health and wellness, along with being a physical and health educator for nearly 20 years. She studied kinesiology and education with a focus on biology, health sciences and physical education at the University of Windsor. Her future plans as an entrepreneur include further developing her life and health coaching business, and real estate. Her studies as of late include a course with Bob Proctor, *Thinking into Results*. Nutrition, exercise and nurturing a healthy mindset are the foundations of her lifestyle. She finds the most reward in helping others unlock and overcome their barriers to live a life they dream of. She is always open minded, open hearted and here to listen and guide you to live your best life.

www.deidreslattery.arbonne.com
ig: Deirdre_slattery | fb: DeidreSlattery

Today, we feel the weight of the world on our shoulders more and more. What is the underlying cause of this? And how is it keeping us from the life we want to live, and move past the life we are living? The word that we all feel - **stress**. It can motivate us to accomplish and achieve great things, yet it can also hold us back from being great. Stress comes at us in so many forms. The pressure to be perfect today is stronger than ever; to be more, to have more and to give more. We are financially stressed, pressed for time, and starved for energy; happiness is low, self-worth is low, family pressures keep surmounting, and the overall expectation is to succeed in society. We expect more and more from ourselves, and society tells us we need to act and look a certain way. When we don't or aren't fitting into the ideal, we adopt it as a limitation. We are constantly judging ourselves, comparing ourselves and worried about how others perceive us. We are expected to be happy with what we have, but still want more! When we are chasing after this ideal of being perfect and feeling less than perfect, we feel like we aren't successful. It is a general anxiety of being disappointed in how we look, act or feel. How can we get to that person we truly desire to become?

"Growing into your future… requires a dedication to caring for yourself as if you were rare and precious, which you are. And regarding all life around you as equally so, which it is." ~ Victoria Moran

A place I have started and come back to in my own journey is body image. From the time I was a young adult, I have worked to maintain and build on a healthy sense of who I am, no matter how complicated and confusing times get throughout all the stages of life. We need to understand what body image means and gain a positive, empowering sense of who we are, and the relationship and connection we feel toward our body, and ultimately our mind. The "I can" motto I am going to share, is a simple tool to create the pattern, and if you choose to dig deeper, rewire your paradigm and belief system around your image. **When you adopt and absorb on a deeper level that you ARE all the amazing qualities you perceive yourself to be, you can then set yourself free to accomplish and evolve into your ideal self.** To do this, we need to let go of past influences that have

41

not been kind to us, and bring all the positive forces and connections in our lives closer to our heart and mind, to strengthen and develop a positive body image.

What Is Your Biggest Dream, And What Is Your Greatest Fear?

Are the two connected? What is our biggest limitation in this world? Most of us would say it is our own selves! We can either be our greatest asset or biggest downfall. The balance in life, and the beautiful connection to our best life - the life we truly dream of, begins when we have taken back who we are, and live the life we desire boldly and bravely.

For years, I taught young adolescent females before having my own daughter, and during that time I could envision for them how unique, talented, and gifted they all are and wished that they too will see their own light, and never lose it. It is human nature to treat each other with respect, kindness, optimism, and hope in their infinite potential for success, and ultimately happiness. I saw this within all these young women, and wish the same for my daughter. We have beaten ourselves up and down, and forgotten the beautiful bright light we once were. To put our career first, our family first, a relationship, the house, the bills, and slowly we have taken a back seat in our own lives. It is when life is cruising along, and suddenly you are taken off course not gently, but rather taken off course tragically or painfully; and all that you hope for and give to others is sometimes much less than you have ever given to your own self. *When did we stop loving ourselves, taking care of ourselves, believing in our greatness, and taking the time to invest in our own well-being?*

We hide in a comfortable status quo, but are uncomfortable within the layers we mask ourselves in. We escape, skip out, miss opportunities, second guess, and procrastinate until it isn't a choice any longer, but has, in fact, become our way of life. We can make excuses and say things like, *I am happy with how I am*, or, *what I have now is good enough*. Why is this? Lack of self-confidence and self-esteem can keep us safely from living out our own dreams and our best life.

Below are some questions to consider your level of self-esteem and body image:

- Do you put off social engagements, activities, jobs, trips, or relationships until you are a certain size or weight?

- Do you feel you would be happy if you were a certain size?

- Would losing or gaining weight make you feel you were a better person?

- Do you think changing a part of your body would make your life better?

- Do you feel guilty about eating certain foods?

- Do you speak of your body negatively or find your thoughts are negative?

- Do you accept and give compliments freely of yourself and to others?

Take a moment to answer these questions, and truly reflect on whether you respect and accept your body, and have a healthy self-image, or, if you need to work on improving and changing your beliefs on body image and self-esteem?

You are not alone if you answered yes to many of these questions, or feel you would like to make a shift in these results to get to a place where you feel good about yourself, and how you feel others perceive you as well. Approximately 90% of women are unhappy with their bodies, which then leads to unrealistic dieting and body goals. The unfortunate fact is that less than 5% of the population is born with the body type that the media portrays as still being desirable or ideal. Body image is closely tied to self-esteem; if one is low, the other follows along with a higher incidence of eating disorders, unhealthy or abusive relationships and sexual activity, substance use, and suicidal thoughts.[4] Striving for an

---

[4]DoSomething.org. (2014, February, 24). 11 Facts about Body Image. Retrieved from https://www.dosomething.org/us/facts/11-facts-about-body-image

ideal body without seeking safe and informed nutritional guidance and support, may lead to unhealthy relationships with food and behaviors. If you are feeling this is ringing true for you, or someone you care about, please seek out professional help, a good place to start is with a family physician.

In the last 20 years, the facts and numbers of women striving for an ideal body have changed so drastically in comparison to body norms and diets, yet the ideal has not changed to reflect this. The ideal body has decreased in weight by 23%, and the average woman has increased 4%.[5] How can we be happy healthy and free with ourselves? We begin with our SELF!

How to begin this journey? Here are some simple steps to better our self-worth and body image:

We can set goals and join a gym, but unless we change how we view ourselves, we cannot fully achieve our greatness. To change our behavior, we first need to change our belief.

It is a daily practice to rewire and shift our beliefs. Start the day with affirmations. Say it out loud, write it down, and repeat this throughout the day. For example, *I am a beautiful, strong, and successful woman!* Write it out 100 times, say it 10 times aloud to the sun shining outside, or the beautiful soul in the mirror. Record it on your phone to listen often throughout the day, and keep a note in your wallet.

While You Are Changing Your Belief! Write Your Future!

Action and activity can reinforce your desired change. Get out of your head, and into the world of doing and being who you are, and what you know you are capable of.

To rewire your brain and your paradigm, also practice journaling, and writing out the life you desire (down to every last detail) in the present tense. Some things to envision and write about clearly are: Who are you surrounding yourself with in your success, at work, and at home?

---

[5]Brumberg, J.J. (1997, August, 19). The Body Project: An Intimate History of American Girls. New York, NY: Random House

Where are you? - is it indoors, outdoors, the beach, city, an apartment, a country home? Envision how it's decorated; the clothes you feel best in, and the look on your face. Visiting the image of who you are becoming and want to be, often drives that confidence level up, and imprints itself in your mind and heart, that **this is you!** Find quotes and apps on your phone to give you some daily inspiration to keep you positive and focused on the good in your life. Center yourself on more than just a physical ideal, or negative comparison you could be beating yourself up over.

Building Body Image - Dress For Success

How you dress is key to success and breaking into the best version of yourself. You want to embrace your beauty, and who you are and show that outwardly to the world you are creating. Think of five of your favorite outfits and how you feel in them. Is this the image you are striving for? You can reinvent your style and your look as often as you need and feel. Part of finding your authentic self is also the confidence to express yourself in the fashion and style you carry yourself in. When you are in your zone, making the promotion, at the top of your company, how do you look? Begin today by being that person! Dress that way, talk that way, and walk into a room with that energy everywhere you go. It is time to lose the clothes that make you feel less than you are, self-conscious, or negative in any way, and choose clothes that give you the self-confidence and image you desire. What you put out there is your vibe.

Attracting Your Tribe With Your Vibe

Surround yourself with people that respect and honor the person you want to be or become. The kind of people we choose to surround ourselves with can either lift us up or enable us to lose ourselves or lower our standards over time. Raise the bar for the quality of people you choose to spend time with, based on similar goals and dreams for successful, happy and healthy life.

Here is an exercise for you: make a list of your strengths, passions, gifts and talent. In the past, what did you love to do, and what were you good at? Do you still do these things currently? Could you do this in your professional or personal life? When we learn new skills and talents, we tap into our creativity and feel capable and accomplished. This positive cycle repeats itself, and we continue to succeed in other areas, lifting our confidence and feeling of self-worth.

You Are Enough! Have You Ever Been Told You Are Too Much?

You are all that you need, and it is inside of you. Bringing that uniqueness out and sharing your passion is also key to unlocking your potential. When we begin to share this and see the ripple effect of it, we also are helping others see and feel their own worth, and we grow together. Shifting our intention from ourselves to helping others remarkably builds our sense of self, and builds our personal esteem.

Body image is a combination of self-image, esteem, and confidence. We can raise all these areas in some of the following ways to better our body image; get active and treat your body like it's a gift to move, dance, run, bike swim, or lift weights. It is only natural to fuel your body with good foods then. More often than not, eating healthy and choosing foods that nourish our bodies and health helps us immensely. The more good we do, the more we deepen the pattern and develop the willpower to treat our bodies and minds with care and nurture our self-love. I like to live by the 80 - 20 rule. It is a rule of thumb for a balanced life that is doable by most. In a given day, and over the period of one week, if we are choosing choices that are bettering our body and mind in regards to meals, exercise, sleep, social commitments and free time 80 % of the time; the other 20 % of the time, we may choose food for other reasons that bring us pleasure such as fun, convenience, social events, or tastings. The goal is to view food and all our choices not as good or bad, but, rather consider the relationship with your choices as positive and healthy. Food, for example, is not a good or bad thing, but a means to take care of our body and health, some of which is social and emotional. Developing a positive relationship with food can be a start to gaining back the joy in eating healthy, and choosing fitness for ourselves and our bodies. Asking the 5 questions when we choose food can be a simple way to get in touch with our eating habits and learn more about food and all its wonderful benefits. When we develop the ability to make healthy choices in how we feed and exercise our body and minds, we are a step closer to becoming the best versions of ourselves, and doing all that we want to do in this lifetime.

Triggers

The 5 questions to consider are: When do we eat? What do we choose to eat? How do we prepare the food? With whom do we eat? And why are we choosing it? Taking time to check in when we eat, exercise, and pick our outfits helps fill our day for any aspect of life. Give yourself room for spontaneity, to live off the charts, and simply have fun with food, life, work, and adventures!

Tracking Your Efforts And Successes

Track it and watch it grow. Schedule your gym dates, check them off every time you make it there. This can be translated to other areas when you have adopted your new routines. The 5 tasks or most important things you want to get done each day to better yourself, can be on a list that you can track and cross off after you have completed them. We can see results in the numbers, and experience the progress. If you set out to go to the gym 3 times a week and do yoga 2 times, and you track your success, it will have a natural effect to motivate you and keep you on course. Celebrate your efforts and successes along your journey and with that, note the improvement in your sense of self. You are stronger, wiser, more competent, happier and healthier. This exudes self-confidence, and is like fuel in the tank to help you keep going for more!

Practicing Gratitude And Giving Back

Again, focus beyond the weight or an ideal body; focus on life, what you are grateful for, and how you can help others. Giving your time, knowledge and attention to others will lift your spirits and feeling of belonging. Take the time to feel this sense of love and gratitude. Maintaining a gratitude journal to begin and end your day is a such a grounding and lifting routine as we have so much right here in our own playgrounds to tend to and care for. Gratitude is fortitude.

We can be our best friend and love ourselves, or we can fall out of love with ourselves, lose the positive vibe we need to feel connected, and become our own worst enemy. Be kind to "yourself," love "yourself" like you would love a child, and if you are a parent, this can be shared with your children along with your own journey now, to empower them for their future.

Take daily steps to break down the limitations you are hiding behind because of a low self-esteem or body image.

Crystal Clear Vision

Create and make a vision so clear of the life you want, and how you are getting there. This vision is so clear, it is a reality, and no-one can get in your way. Make it happen when you decide you are your greatest ally, you are your greatest gift and talent, and you are more than that!

When we break down *why* we have a poor image of ourselves, we can rewrite them and replace them with positive and powerful images to step into our ideal self and not just a body. Rewrite your script. Burn and cast away the negative self-talk and the ideas that have been planted in your head. **Let it go.**

Embrace yourself as a whole person and see your light; share it and foster it! Your light is needed in the world, and you make a difference to others.

"When you are living the best version of yourself you inspire others to live the best versions of themselves."~ Steve Maraboli

Chapter 4

Embracing Personal Style, Comfort & Fashion Confidence

by Shelbi De Silva

"I have always believed that fashion was not only to make women more beautiful, but also to reassure them, give them confidence."
~ Yves Saint Laurent

Shelbi De Silva

Shelbi De Silva is a small town girl who has made her way into the corporate fashion industry. Her experience is rooted in fashion, identity and consumer culture. She works for a major Canadian fashion brand, and is passionate about both the retail and style aspects of the business. Her chapter explores how brands, styles, and trends impact a woman's sense of style, fashion identity, and confidence.

In her academic career, Shelbi studied popular culture at Brock University, obtaining a BA and MA in the field. In her research, she focused on critical aspects of fashion, advertising, and personal styling. She has also volunteered at Toronto Fashion Week runway shows, and has worked on the sales floor for popular women's clothing brands for seven years before moving into a corporate fashion merchandising role.

Shelbi is passionate about encouraging women to embrace the best versions of themselves through fashion. She believes that through fashion, woman can find empowerment through what they choose to wear, regardless of societal position.

ig: sherob

Advertising and branding invade Western culture and contribute to society's "needs," wants, desires, social values, identities, ideals, and fantasies. Fashion styles and clothing are powerful sources of emotional and meaningful identity construction, even though they work within and produce class paradoxes. In the fashion industry, a complex system of power relations exists. An individual's fashion choices can reflect class and social position, as well as taste. For women's fashion specifically, the media industry and popular culture dictate "this season's hottest trends," "how to dress for your body type," or "how to get a look for less." There is a complicated relationship that surrounds fashion, identity, taste, and consumption. Fashion has the potential to create a space for originality or conformity, and experimentation is endless for a modern consumer. For the modern day woman, who may be working a corporate 9-5 while simultaneously being a mom, a wife, maybe working towards a school degree or working as an entrepreneur, dressing in a way that works for your lifestyle, while also for comfort can be an overwhelming challenge. In today's fashion industry, popular trends and looks are mainly catered to a "mainstream" body type and style taste, and the marketplace is filled with a mix of luxury, as well as fast fashion. In recent years, the introduction of plus-size fashions, social media accounts like @Effyourbeautystandards, and promotion of The Body Positive Movement[6] has created a conversation about inclusivity and self-acceptance within the fashion industry. On that note, I would like to share some of my ideas and tips on how to embrace one's personal style, comfort, and fashion confidence.

Fashion Roots

Growing up in a small, country town did not offer exposure to much diversity in any form, including races and cultures, style and fashion. Some (including my now husband) may describe my sociocultural learnings in adolescence as "sheltered," as I cannot claim to have eaten international cuisines at friends' houses, or being familiar with different cultural dress and customs. Since most of the people

---

[6]The Body Positive (1996). Retrieved from http://www.thebodypositive.org

I grew up with were from heterosexual, white, middle-class, average-bodied families, most of them had the same interests which ended up resulting in the same type of personal style and fashion. This "type" wore simple looks featuring popular brands and put together an overall conservative look. I think my now fascination with consumer taste, fashion and style come from this overall lack of exposure to different fashion styles growing up.

As a pre-teen, I remember getting my first magazine subscription. Every month, I would eagerly get the magazine from the mailbox, and read it front to back in one night. Articles such as, "What is your personal style?" or, "How to update your wardrobe on a budget!" filled and duplicated themselves across issues with slight tweaks. I would only ever read an article once, but I was obsessed with the images and advertising in the magazines. My mother will attest, that when I was 15, I had all four of my bedroom walls covered in magazine ads and editorial images. I taped up anything that I thought looked cool, and it became my bedroom wall art. I stared at the images all the time. Being plus-size, I knew that I could never pull off some of the fashion looks from the magazines, but I was still intrigued by the colors and textures in the images. With the popularity of social media, and positive body image models such as Ashley Graham, Tess Holliday and Hunter McGrady in today's fashion industry, it is interesting to think of how this would've impacted me as a teenager, and how I approached my personal style and fashion sense.

Finding Your Style

After focusing my schooling within the discourses of fashion, I moved from the country to the cosmopolitan and felt more exposed to non-traditional clothing and style. I knew from my early pre-teen years that I would eventually make my way to the big city and work in the fashion industry, which is where I am now. The city represents a place of unique fashion tastes, as it is a chaotic space full of strangers where each one wants to differentiate oneself. I believe I appreciate others' fashion and personal style more than the average person, as I find it intriguing to analyze someone's fashion and style choices. My personal style is quite plain, but I do like to dabble with trends and take risks. Comfort drives my style; thus something may look good on me, but if it is digging into my stomach or riding up my legs, I don't want to wear it. I know the feeling I get when I am wearing something uncomfortable, and it will completely affect my mood. On the other hand, when I am wearing something I feel comfortable in, I feel more naturally confident in my day. I think there is a misconception of what is "professional" or "unprofessional." For example, one may say that a skirt suit is an essential part of a business woman's wardrobe, however, in my opinion, wearing anything that constricting (especially with pantyhose underneath) is a true fashion crime. I don't think style is sacrificed just because something is comfortable. Note – I am not endorsing sweatpant wearing to the office! I am a firm believer that if you like something, wear it, without dwelling on what others will think. Working in a corporate office has given me an interesting exposure to how the modern working woman dresses for a business meeting. My office dress code is pretty casual; for the most part, you will find me in jeans with a sweater or top. Some women dress in dresses and skirts with pantyhose on a daily basis. It becomes evident that certain women feel comfortable and empowered wearing certain pieces. However, for me, since I dress so casual on a daily basis, when I do have to dress up for a meeting or presentation, it does not necessarily mean I need to be in a dress or a skirt to look professional. I can wear a nice pair of dress pants with a blazer and an edgy flat and still have a clean, professional (and trendy) look. A blazer is definitely an empowering piece that every woman should own in her closet - it can transform the look of a basic tee and jeans!

Females have interesting shopping patterns and mentalities. There are some that are addicted to shopping, always wanting the newest thing; there are some that go shopping for themselves once a year; there are some that invest in expensive pieces and have few, and there are some that spend money on fast fashion and are constantly updating their wardrobe. Some of these mentalities are driven by needs, wants, finances, and others are driven by a desire to be refreshing and updating one's style identity constantly. Throughout my twenties, my shopping style evolved tremendously. I used to buy anything I liked and wanted, and then after years of doing this, I realized how many unnecessary items my closet had accumulated, and spent a good year purging about five years worth of this habit. I got rid of many items that still had tags or that I wore once, it was a cathartic process! I realized that I bought many of these items because I was attracted to them, but in reality, they were not comfortable on me, and I would not feel comfortable wearing them. I am now a more budget conscious spender and am more honest with myself about whether I really need the item, and if I will wear it. I mainly shop sale items and do a lot of online window shopping, so I don't make impulse purchases. I think part of my bad habits came from always working in the mall or a retail space and having such easy access to purchase items. Now, I stay out of malls and usually shop with a friend so they can restrain me and help provide a voice of reasoning - "Shelbi - you have something like that already in your closet!"

Trying To Fit (In)

I worked on the sales floor in Women's fashion retail for 7 years before moving into the corporate fashion world, and in that time I interacted with so many different women. When I reflect on some of my customer service experiences in retail, I think about the comments and conversations I had with them, which helped drive their buying decisions. Consistently, customers would take a variety of items into the fitting room, and come out each time to look at themselves in the mirror. As part of my job, I would ask politely, "What do you think?" and customer responses were consistently started with, "I like it but…" followed by something like:

- "… I don't think I can pull it off"

- "… Don't you think it accentuates my butt / shoulders / stomach?"

- "… I don't think my boyfriend / husband will like it"

- "… What do you think?"

Through these "in-field" observations, it became very apparent that fashion & dress are definitely areas in which societal constraints and expectations dictate and form a woman's identity. It also becomes glaring how non-confident women are in deciding on their fashion choices. Over the years, this became very annoying to me. As a generally confident, comfortable in my own skin type of person, I had such a hard time understanding the self-deprecating thought process that went through a woman's head, when deciding if she wanted to buy a $29 top. She was obviously attracted to it to pick it up off the rack and take into the fitting room, and I can understand if right away she put it on and said, "Nope not for me." However, I still have a hard time understanding the decision process before deciding to buy, based on the what if, or what will others think mentality. Some questions I ask myself when shopping that has helped build my fashion confidence are thinking about things like:

- *Why am I attracted to this item? Is it because I've seen it in ads everywhere or because I saw someone else wearing it and thought it was great?*

- *Whose style am I attracted to and why? What pieces do wear a lot that I love and need?*

- *Am I comfortable in this? Will I wear it and not feel I have to constantly adjust, pick, and pull at this item as I wear it?*

You Are What You Wear

Thus, a woman's fashion decisions are unfortunately dictated by societal norms, as opposed to personal desire, comfort or taste. Although the mainstream media is far from celebrating every body type as equally beautiful, attractive and normal, there has been slow, yet positive progress over the last couple years. Now, when I pick up a magazine, I see diverse, realistic body types gracing the pages. There are plus-size, athletic, and non-traditional models featured on major magazine covers celebrating the diversity of women's bodies. Although the media dictates societal norms in the fashion world, I think the embracing of oneself, and being confident in fashion purchase choices is the responsibility of consumers. Females need to voice their opinions with their buying power, and feel confident (and most importantly, *comfortable!*) doing so!

Chapter 5

Say No So You Can Say Yes

by Shabira Wahab

"When you say 'yes' to others, make sure you are not saying 'no' to yourself." ~ Paulo Coelho

Shabira Wahab

After graduating with a BA in psychology from York University, Shabira knew she did not want to become a psychologist and felt like there was something different out there for her. She wanted to find her true calling. She started a few businesses, but never felt like they were her passion. She wanted to help people but didn't know how.

After surviving an abusive relationship in her twenties, Shabira thought she had got past the worst, but it took years for her to rebuild her self-worth. Finally starting to find herself and accept herself at the age of 30, Shabira knew she wanted to start helping women specifically. She wanted to help them know their worth, accept themselves for who they are, and get out of bad relationships and began taking coaching courses geared specifically towards women's empowerment. It was here that she realized she had found her passion. Shabira is now passionate about helping women find their sparkle.

Shabira loves that she grew up in Toronto where she was exposed to many ethnicities, cultures, and religions. She loves traveling to new places where she can learn about the different cultures of the world. As an open-minded and non-judgmental person, Shabira loves learning about people and hearing their life stories.

ig: _yousparkle_ | fb: YouSparkle

We Are Not In This World To Live Up To Others' Expectations

Most women dream of having the perfect relationship. A relationship where we are respected and treated as a partner. A relationship where we can voice our opinions and be heard. However, even those of us who dream of these relationships, do not always end up in these ideal situations. We know what we want, but we don't express it. Sometimes, this is due to the expectations we feel we have to live up to. The expectation of being a good girlfriend or wife. The expectation that a good relationship is free of conflict; that both partners should always want the same things and do the same things at all times.

"Living up to the expectations of our partners is not always possible. Moreover, living up to the expectations of our partners should not always be expected." ~ Shabira Wahab

Expectations can make it extremely difficult to say no to a partner. When it came to saying no within a relationship, I used to get all flustered and had a lot of difficulty doing it. Whether I did not want to do something as simple as going out to meet him after a long day at work, or something as big as lending a significant amount of money, I didn't know how to simply stay true to myself and say no. I wanted to please, and avoid conflict and confrontation. I would worry that by saying no, he would get hurt or angry, and I would then be seen as a bad girlfriend. I would just go along with things like *nothing was wrong*, when in fact, everything was wrong. As a survivor of an emotionally and mentally abusive relationship, I had to rebuild my self-worth. It took the understanding that my self-worth was already low before the relationship, and would remain low unless I enforced change. Through time and inner reflection, I've gotten over this need to live up to others expectations. If someone wants to get upset or end a relationship simply for saying no to them, then good riddance to them! I will gladly hold the door open for them on their way out. I want other women to get over this need, too. I hear other women's stories and their complaints of having to cater to their partner with no reciprocation. Living just to meet the expectations of others, sucks. It's no way to live. Live to meet your own expectations. Relationships, new or old, are a two-way street where both partners have an equal say, and should feel comfortable asking for what they want.

Reasons we may be afraid to say no to our partner:

- Social / family pressures – traditional thinking, *You're the woman, you should do as your man says.*

- Upbringing - as children, women are expected to always be nice and helpful; which can turn us into adults who are eager to please, and saying no means you are a bad person.

- Mirrored behavior - Has anyone ever told you, "You're just like your mother?" There's a reason for that.

- Need to please.

- Afraid your partner will leave if you do not live up to their expectations.

- We think it will make the relationship better.

My issues with saying no can be mainly attributed to both my upbringing as a female, and mirrored behavior. As little girls, we are expected to *always be nice* and that we should constantly be helping others. This turns us into women who are eager to please and feel bad about saying no because that means we are a bad person... Growing up, I would see my mother doing so much for others, and never really taking time for herself or saying no to something when she was too busy. Instead, she would say yes, and complain about it later. The thinking that saying yes and agreeing to everything will make the relationship better is completely wrong. This leads to resentment and opens you up to being treated like a doormat. What I've learned is that saying no does not mean I'm a bad person. It doesn't always have to mean a flat out no, either; it can also mean *compromise*. Saying no means *standing up for yourself*. It means valuing you, your wants, and your boundaries enough to say something. So how do you break out of this limiting behavior and learn to say no?

Give Yourself The Love & Permission To Change

Everyone is allowed to change. We often hear that, *"people never change."* This is not something I believe. People change all the time. They just have to want to change and realize that they NEED to change. Once you give yourself permission to change, you will realize learning to say no is a way of growing and empowering yourself.

Understand That There May Be Push Back To Your Change

Your partner has been conditioned and is accustomed to you behaving a certain way. They may not like that you are trying to grow, or it may cause a misunderstanding. Practice saying no; think about a situation that comes up when you tend to give in and think of how you will say no instead. This will help you with any pushback you may receive.

Speak Your Mind, RESPECTFULLY. Now, This Step Is Two-Fold

A) This means saying what you want; standing up for yourself. You want to do this without putting your partner down. Let them know you understand their position. Avoid folding your arms, or any body language that can come off as defensive or closed. Again, practice. Practice in private, and then be sure to voice your opinion as often as possible. The more you do it, the more natural it will become. B) This could also mean explaining to your partner that you are trying to change. It means saying that you do not like your people pleasing ways, and are trying to grow, take care of yourself, and feel better about yourself. Your partner may worry that this means they will no longer have your constant support. This is when it is important to let them know you will be there to support them as much as they are there to support you. You're not trying to change the relationship but rather, you're trying to grow the relationship.

Discussion Doesn't Always Mean No

This simply means looking for ways to compromise and meet each other halfway. There is always a way to compromise. He wants to go out tonight, but you don't? Make a deal to reschedule for another night, or suggest some things you can do at home instead.

Let Guilt Go!

This can be a tough one, and can often resurface. As women, we were raised to *want to please* our partners and meet all of their expectations. If we don't go along with what they say, we feel bad and then question how we are good partners. Bull! **By learning how to say no, you are healing yourself.** You are growing into a better person, and there is never anything wrong with that. Part of letting go of guilt comes from an understanding of why you feel guilty. Sit down and think about **where** this emotion is coming from. Is it something you saw in your childhood? The relationship dynamics between your own parents? A cultural belief? Find the cause, and tell yourself there's no need to feel guilty about bettering yourself and becoming a stronger person.

Managing The Feedback

If you're receiving negative feedback to your growth, or even angry / violent outbursts, consider whether you're in a healthy relationship. While there are thousands of situations where you can compromise, think about what your partner is asking of you. Are they trying to guilt you into having sex? Are they making you feel bad for not giving them money? This could be an indication that you're in an unhealthy, possibly emotionally abusive, relationship. This is a whole other topic which deserves an entire book to be addressed. Put simply, please seek assistance and get out of any abusive relationship. Outside of abusive relationships, saying no can actually strengthen your relationship. You'll have a new-found sexy respect for yourself, and your partner should, too. It will set boundaries, and show you and your partner how to respect each other's boundaries. This empowers you and teaches your partner to do the same, leading to a stronger relationship in which both partners are true - not just to each other, but to themselves.

Section 2

The Past Is Not A Limit

Featuring

Emily Marie Gruzinski, Jess Arbour, Cindi Melkerson, Lisa Gartly, and Katherine Debs

Opening commentary by Ky-Lee Hanson

As women, we have the common experience of growing up with an unfair advantage within a patriarchal society. Some of us experience worse circumstances than others depending on political and religious differentiations between countries. In our modern and historical society, no matter the country, we have experienced being the lesser of two. Throughout history, there have been women's movements and I ask myself, are we still *moving* or are we now standing and demanding? I feel 2016 was a year where we began to call shots. Maybe it is because of my age and greater awareness that I am noticing it more, but things feel different. We are not the weak gender, and are tired of false stereotypes being portrayed onto us.

We are not going to take it anymore. In the last section, we discussed some all too common limitations women experience around body image and social standards, within relationships, and running a household. Today, men are beginning to stay home with the children and magazines too, have depicted a way a man should look. It's not ok. For women, it has been the only life we have known, and that is what we are discussing here in this book. Where and when did we learn these limits we are now pushing past? Were we completely hopeless and naive at some point, or were we conditioned by our ancestors and society? Either way, the past cannot repeat itself.

Growing up, children are influenced by the boxes they are put in; gender, location, physical ability or inabilities, the financial class of their family and the colour of their skin. People are also judged based on how quickly they learn, the grades they achieve *including subjects of no interest or of less personal use*, and how well they follow rules - sit down, put your head down, no using the washroom, drinking water or eating during class, speak only when spoken to or when your raised hand is acknowledged. We grow up under predefined circumstances, riddled with expectations of our limits and abilities.

The women in this book decided to not let their past circumstances control, design, or limit their life. We wonder, what is possible and how can *we* get there? This is where we begin. Emily starts off this section with her story of triumph, self belief, and proving the past does not define you. Jess continues to look at circumstances but from the limited view through isolation. If you cannot see it, can it be? Do we accept our circumstances and environment as all there is? Do we accept our past or present, as our fate? How much blame do we put on our surroundings, which hinders and limits us? We must be extremely aware of what we accept into our personal world. Or maybe we have accepted an uncomfortable and mediocre life as "our reality"- as our world. Can we change a limited mind to an abundant mind? Cindi will take us through that journey. What if you feel, and have accepted that you do not have resources, or are not good enough to receive them? You have forgotten what you know to be true - you forgot your unique worth. Luckily, it is never too late to flip the coin, take a chance. *But, oh no, what are people going to think?!* Change and taking a chance - taking a stance - is never easy. Lisa will help us to learn what it is to live in our sweet spot, how to deflect negativity and come out stronger. Katherine shows us strength from excelling past civil war, women in-equality, stigmas in career and helps us be aware of our strong female intuition; to trust it. Our message is, you do not have to accept unideal circumstances as a way of life.

Chapter 6

Past Does Not Define You

by Emily Marie Gruzinski

"The past is like an anchor holding us back.
You have to let go of who you are to become who you will be."
~ Unknown

Emily Marie Gruzinski

Emily is from a small town in the suburbs of Colorado. She is a wine lover, dog lover, part introvert, college dropout, and travel enthusiast. She met her husband on the pristine coast of Florida and later moved to Maryland, where she currently resides. Her warm, patient, yet relentless and enthusiastic personality has allowed her to deal with the high stresses that come in life and the new changes that arrive, with poise and ease.

In her earlier years, growing up wasn't always easy, it was very challenging at times; from nearly losing her mother, to being evicted from her home as a family due to financial stresses, she didn't want to let her past define her, and kept her eye on the future. Wanting to make her footprint on the world and desiring to feel a deep sense of making an impact, she realized it's all about the mindset, and that anyone can change the direction of their future with one simple step.

She took action towards changing her destiny, and it has led her on a path to entrepreneurial freedom.

Refusing to let any setbacks get in her way, she is passionate about helping others realize the same. Everyone has baggage and that it is ok. No matter what yours looks like, you are still a person whose dreams should be realized. She is the kind of person who will help you realize your full potential, and is living proof that the past does not define your future.

ig: GskiAdventures | fb: Emily Wood Gruzinski

Have you ever had that burning desire that you know you are worth more in life but not sure what the next step is or if you are even worth it? What is holding / limiting you back? Is it the fear of failure, or is it starting something new and having it ripped out from under you, again? Pretending to be someone that you aren't? Fear of getting out of your comfort zone and reaching your true potential? Worried about what others think? Have you ever let judgments or criticism from your past hinder who you are in the present? Perhaps the root of it all is that you are deeply affected by your past experiences, and this is carried with you into the future and affects your choices. Now is the time to take back that power.

Some people have had an extremely tough childhood, perhaps they were teased, hurt by a loved one, even lost a loved one, had a traumatic incident, lived in poverty, or had no support or positive influences in their life. The good news is the past does not define you; you define yourself.

We see so many people dogged by their past. They live in their failures or success.

Think about the jock from high school who is still out partying, and trying to live the life of the typical all-star athlete. The only problem is, he's no longer 18 and in top physical shape. No, in reality, he's the 40-year-old who has a beer belly and health problems. He's an alcoholic who cannot stop drinking. It's a sad sight.

Or there's the beauty pageant mom who never won the crown. Now she's parading her children around, wanting them to be on the next TLC's *Toddlers and Tiaras* show; yet on the inside, she is still unfulfilled.

Unfortunately, these people have let their past define them. They are still trying to live the life they lived years ago. The truth is, we don't have to let the past define us. We can move on from our past into something better. It is the power of our thinking that can either limit us or take us to our full potential. The choice is yours.

Get Over The Past

One of the first steps in reaching your full potential is to not worry about your past. It may have helped shape you, but holding onto grudges or experiences that didn't go the way you wanted to, should not define your future. The only way you can accept new joy and happiness into your life is to make space for it. If your heart is filled to the brim with pain and hurt, how can you be open to anything new? Make the decision to let it go. Things don't disappear on their own. You need to make the commitment to let it go. If you don't make this conscious choice up-front, you could end up self-sabotaging any effort to move on from this past hurt.

Making the decision to let it go also means accepting you have a choice to let it go - to stop reliving the past pain, to stop going over the details of the story in your head every time you think of the other person or experience. Whether you went through a traumatic situation, or someone else was involved, express your pain verbally and get it out of your system. If you cannot talk to someone directly about it, vent to a friend; write it in a journal, but get it all out of your system. By doing so, you will gain an understanding of specifically where your hurt is stemming from, and what it's about. Vent, forgive, and focus on the now; now is the time to let go. Let go of the past, and stop reliving it. All you can do is make today the best day of your life.

Nobody's life should be defined by their pain. It's not healthy, it adds to our stress, it hurts our ability to focus, study and work, and it impacts every other relationship we have. Every day you choose to hold on to the pain, is another day everybody around you has to live with that decision. And feel its consequences.

So do everybody - and yourself - a big favor: let go of the pain. Do something different today, and welcome happiness back into your life.

I'll always remember my childhood; it was filled with wholesome memories, strolling to the neighborhood park with our dogs; dancing around the living room; my father waking me up on a warm summer morning and surprising us with an exciting, spontaneous trip to the amusement park. Life definitely had its warm fuzzy moments, and then also the not so good ones. Normal, right? Yes. Life was not easy growing up. My mother was a nurse, and my father worked in construction. I witnessed them working around the clock;

their work ethic was inspiring. Our family bond was strong, and our love was unbreakable, but on the inside, we were really struggling financially. So much so, that as I was walking up to my home from middle school on a cloudy spring day, I suddenly saw several big men walking in and out of our home with their hands full. I was confused, did we have company? I saw them go in empty handed, and out with as many items as they could carry. I sobbed to my mother, "What is going on, mom?" We were being evicted from my childhood home. It was devastating and embarrassing seeing all our personal belongings on our front lawn. Tears streaming down my face as everything I owned was being tossed into large black trash bags and tossed onto the front yard. I'll never forget having a neighbor come over. I don't remember who she was, but I remember clear as day, this sweet old lady came and sat next to me on the front lawn as I was somewhat sorting through things, and trying to keep my composure at age twelve when I came across my favorite butterfly necklace. While attempting to untangle the necklace, the woman looked at me and said, "My dear, remember, out of any ugly situation becomes something beautiful." It was stuck with me for life. She was the only one able to see the light in the dark.

After that disheartening day, we moved several times, switching schools, trying to start over repeatedly, trying to get back on our feet. It appears the end was so far. I admired my parents for never giving up and having faith that things would work out, and deep down I knew I had to carry that same belief. Not long after, my mother also became extremely ill with mercury poisoning, to the nature that we did not think she would survive my younger years. I couldn't believe it was happening; my rock, I needed her more than ever during that time, but I refused to let my entire world crumble down on me. I kept my head held high, and one foot in front of the other. My parents needed me to stay strong. My father did not stop working; we were all there for each other, but life was tough back then. Did we stop moving forward? No. Did we consistently fight? Yes. Was it stressful? Absolutely. No matter how unbearable it seemed at times, no matter how hard it was to see the light at the end of the tunnel, we did not give up, we had to be grateful we had each other, and time was eventually on our side. My mother started to get better slowly, and we found a high school where I could complete all four years in and not switch schools again. The point that I want to share is that I could have let my past define me.

When my mother was sick, I could have run away, gotten into sex, drugs, alcohol, become depressed, and gone down the wrong path, but I chose not to. I had to face fear. I had faith that a good future will come, that we will get through the tough times, and that the future was bright and will be. Keeping those positive thoughts in my head for years has taught me so much - to be patient, diligent, persistent, and that everything always does work out, with the right attitude and action. We are never given anything that we cannot truly handle. Everyone has their own deck of cards handed to them; the question is, will you play the right card next and decide to pass and not fight? What if you got a royal flush? The choice is yours. No matter your history, no matter your past; you have the choice to let it build you, but don't let it define you.

Throughout the following 10 years, I learned to keep my head held high and pushed through the stressful times because I knew that I could get through anything after experiencing the emotional and financial trauma as a child. However, once in my twenties, I realized that I needed a change in my life. Life was treating me well, but things were too consistent; it was comfortable. I was happily engaged then to my boyfriend of 8 years and now husband, we had a beautiful home together and a loving family, and traveled the world. I was on a successful career path, but I felt that something was missing. I longed to have the opportunity for flexibility, freedom, fulfillment, and to discover it on my own. To spread my wings. To have a purpose. To know that what we went through had a purpose. How could I achieve my full potential? It was scary to realize that someone can work so hard on building something and then have it be swept right out from under them. So why try and build something grand? Well, I did not want to be even close to experiencing those feelings I felt when my family had $20 to their name again. Thoughts trembled through my mind - *Was I good enough? Am I meant for more? How could I find a solution to make our future even better? And where did I need to start?* I wanted our future family to have endless possibilities and opportunities. Was I afraid to fail? Yes. But fear is just proof that it is real, and that the only way to really fail is to quit.

One afternoon, I aimlessly came across an entrepreneurial opportunity. I was intrigued to learn more. I had no idea what it was or how it could change my life, but something about it was compelling. I could almost taste the freedom of owning my own time, being my own boss, and loved the sense of having control of my future. I decided to learn more about the opportunity, dig deep into some research, and see what this was all about. What did I have to lose? As I learned more about it, I found out that I would have to talk to a lot of people! Something I wasn't too comfortable with. The thought of going out more into the world, and completely going out of my comfort zone, worrying about what others thought, made my stomach feel like it was in a million knots. *Was I capable of this? Was I going to be good enough?* Those thoughts lingered in my head for a couple of days. But something kept this opportunity constantly in my mind. I felt the fire inside me grow; perhaps it was my chance to shine and prove to the world that anyone can do what you put your mind to. I refused to let my past experience keep me in that comfort zone; it shaped me, but it does not define me. I thought about this door opening all day, and all night. As nervous as I was, as unsure I may have been at that time, I saw the hope that I needed to be free, the opportunity to be able to live the life that we have always dreamed of - how could I pass that up? I got over myself; I kept those positive thoughts in my head and ran with it. *I am worthy. I am successful. I am smart. I am confident.* My morning mantra. I got out of my comfort zone. One and half years later, it has changed our lives in more ways than one. Not only have we been able to become debt free with this business, and gained the confidence I had deep down inside; it has allowed us to dream big again, to become deeply passionate about now helping others get on their path to financial freedom and to open up incredible opportunities!

Working on yourself is key to any success. Learning from the past, not letting it hold you back, and instead using it as fuel, will drive you so far, you'll look back and realize it was all strangely meant to be. Now, you may be faced with a decision coming up, a big one, just know that it is ok to get out of your comfort zone, it is healthy to do so. We all have to do it from time to time, so just do it. Overall, the journey in this business has taught me so many things - that despite the struggles I had growing up until high school, and though I dropped out of college - that no matter what your background is, you CAN reach your goals, you CAN change your situation, and you absolutely CAN be successful! Change your mindset to a positive one and amazing things will happen.

Reaching Your True Potential And Getting Out Of The Comfort Zone

Having doubts or worrying is normal, but the key lies in not allowing it to consume you. It's a matter of shifting your mindset to a positive outlook. Your mind is everything, don't let the past affect your future. Don't let your past dictate your future. If you're not fulfilled, change it. If you're not feeling well, change it. If you feel that there is something more out there for you and that you haven't' reached it yet, know that it will come; you'll have to jump out of your comfort zone, but it will help you grow to your full potential. Don't limit yourself. Many people limit themselves to what they think they can do. You can go as far as your mind lets you. What you believe, remember, you can achieve.

We will always all be learning and growing, and it takes some getting used to getting out of your comfort zone, but baby steps are better than no steps. It will extremely be worth it and can open so many other doors for you and your family. So, start with yourself, forget the past, and know that it's over with. Take care of yourself, your body, your mind. Reach high, and you will exceed your own expectations. Regardless of how much light or darkness we have in our past, we cannot allow our past to define us.

Everyone Has Baggage

Since we are human, it is not always easy to instantly deflect how certain words and experiences make us feel, but we can search within ourselves to recognize when they become detrimental to who we are, and how we live our lives and to move forward in a positive way.

Everyone has baggage. Everyone has a past. No matter what yours looks like, you are still a person whose dreams should be realized. Someone who deserves to be loved. A person whose life purpose - whatever it is - is important to humankind. Don't let lingering negative feelings about what happened to you in the past limit who you can be in the future. Remind yourself that you're amazing. Keep your blinders on, and go after your goals because we are all meant for such a wonderful life, and are put on earth for a reason, so reach high my dear! The world is waiting for your full potential! Now go kick-ass.

Chapter 7

It's Not Me, It's My Imperfect Circumstances

by Jess Arbour

"Just as the hand, held before the eye, can hide the tallest mountain, so the routine of everyday life can keep us from seeing the vast radiance and the secret wonders that fill the world."
~ Chasidic saying, eighteenth century

Jess Arbour

"I live to conceptualize a vision, actualize a dream, support and encourage, collaborate and inspire... see the world." ~ Jess Arbour

Jess Arbour is adventurous and full of wonderment in every step she takes; focused and driven, with a contagious optimistic approach and unwavering commitment to helping others achieve ultimate success.

Jess has an insatiable desire to make every minute count. She believes life is about the journey, not the destination. Her bucket list is best described as a bottomless chasm, and as a result, Jess has chosen to design a career that does not tie her to bricks and mortar, and instead allows unrestricted global diversity. In essence, she cherishes a passport full of stamps and not a house full of stuff.

Over the last eight years, Jess has worked on motor yachts as a chief stewardess, inspiring and leading the hospitality department to orchestrate the leisure time of the world's most elite guests. Her experience with working in a team that is thrust into isolated and restricted environments, always in closed quarters, honed her passion to mentor and coach others on how to address mental, cultural and physical challenges. Jess believes these concentrated experiences allow her to better understand and empathize with the experiences most anyone could feel in their day to day life.

Jess's career now focuses on personal development, leadership, and mentoring; expanding and unleashing the true potential for success, while building strong skills with a focus on compassion, patience and genuine respect for plurality in perception's facades.

www.jessicamadeline.com
ig: jessica_madelines

I believe that the biggest limit I have, I created. Yes, I believe I created it. It's not actually real; it has developed over time from perceptions of the dreamer mind of my youth. It was created through the belief that my potential was infinite and would be quickly recognized (and sought after), once in the ideal circumstances. The circumstances that build from creative influences, precise geographical location, specific and direct intellectual stimulation, unrestricted financial backing, the list goes on; essentially, ideal circumstances.

Do any of you recall your last months in high school? Just knowing you were bound for a great and accomplished life? Graduation and the future hung on the horizon like a piñata stuffed with diamonds, gold, adventure and unlimited possibilities; you can hear your kindergarten teacher reciting words from Dr. Seuss's *Oh The Places You'll Go.*

Instead, 17 years since graduating high school, my (self-proclaimed) "remarkable" skills have yet to be fully realized. What has been realized? Excuses. They have woven their narrative unconsciously into my life, as I hear myself explaining (to myself): "It's not me, it's my circumstances." Inspired by the expectations created by looking around to see those who have done it better. So where does that leave me? In a corner built with a wall of justified excuses, and nailed together with a comparison to others who I view as having greater success at this stage in life. It sounds like an exceptionally constructed perfect storm for insecurity and inaction. Great. Good. Wonderful.

I Feel Like I'm Alone, Lost At Sea

Imagine, bobbing in the middle of the Atlantic Ocean, in a 200-foot boat, above water 5000 meters deep, and the nearest shore is roughly 1800 nautical miles in any direction. Sound isolating? Perhaps more isolating than you could ever comprehend; lost at sea. Now imagine you are sitting in the middle of your office, your living room, or a busy restaurant with your closest friends. Can the middle of the ocean and the living room feel like the same place? Bobbing in the center of a vast expanse, nothing to reach out to? Isolation is fully accepting of all; it has no prejudice and no parameters.

Anyone anywhere can feel isolated; it's an incredibly excellent muse for excuses. Being isolated in my twenties was all about feeling like I had so much to offer, but no one to lead me to greatness. There was incredible uncertainty, a constrained existence, and a desire to blow the status quo of life experiences out of the water.

During this time, I was presented with an incredible opportunity, a chance to change my circumstances, and work for some of the most wealthy and successful people in the world - I pounced. Change your circumstances, change the possibilities, right? I set out to build a career on luxury super yachts. *Super yachts*, surely the break of a lifetime! The words super and yacht side by side! My first job, a 200-foot luxury motor yacht for a very (and I mean very) wealthy family. I showed up to the dock on a Sunday evening - new job - new home - new opportunities. I gawked at the wonder of it; eyes wide, head was thrown back, peering up the way you do when you stare up at your favorite uncle as a kid; thinking surely, he is the strongest, tallest man alive. I gazed up at this lavish extravagance looming above me like a foreign animal to be marvelled at, but not tamed. I dragged my worldly possessions in my 50-pound suitcase behind me, my mind reeling with the wonder of it all. I set foot on my new 200-foot job, and home. *Oh, the places I would go!*

The crew entrance door seal decompressed - sounding like something out of a science fiction spacecraft. I was nonchalantly greeted by a crew member and showed to my (shared), an eight-foot by an eight-foot cabin. I stood in the small space with no natural light or fresh air. Instantly, I felt a million miles away from the city, just behind the thin layer of aluminum hull. Ok, here we go, new life, new chances, new possibilities.

Days later, we set sail for my first season in the Caribbean. Between the seasickness, and the watch duties as we bobbed along - no land in sight - came the realization that I couldn't even go for a walk. No more impromptu lunches or weekend workshops. As the years sailed by (ya, I like puns), the dialogue in my head would rattle around, *If only I had more influence from academic minds,* or *I wish I could take more courses,* or *If only I worked in an office with inspiring mentors,* or *If only my peers were interested in similar things.* I felt isolated in so many ways. From a lack of access to regular fitness / gym classes (excuse), from a lack of access to interest groups (excuse), and from the lack of stimulation of having a powerful boss (excuse). What was really missing was a community, but what was extremely present, were excuses. I considered myself (even as I sailed around the world to exceptional locations) as isolated; restricted in opportunity, mentorship and inspiration.

Isolation, Just Another Word For Routine

How did I get this far and accomplish so little? Have you ever said this to yourself quietly, while you are faced with the realization that your daily life is, well, your actual life? Do you wonder, *How did this happen? I should be farther down the track by now. I had big plans.* Wait, plan is probably the wrong word - a plan leads to action steps. With a plan, any excuse would be mere chatter, not barriers; better to say I had big dreams / lots of confidence.

So, at 35, I review all those dreams unrealized and I must ask, what was this self-validated excuse? I unknowingly built a belief that the *right situation* had not presented itself, but it surely would, so just keep waiting. Certainly, I would find my calling- or even better, it would find me. All that was needed was the right circumstances, the right inspiration, the right mentor or community. Then, BAM! My super special calling would be presented without much effort, and with all the opportunity I deserved.

It's worth noting, I've never been afraid of hard work, and spent my 20's working long hours at little more than minimum wage. In hindsight, this was the perfect setup for a decade of well-practiced mediocracy, hoping something would emerge and stir my passion and guide me to great achievements.

Note to our twenty-something readers - this time goes by fast, and much more quickly if the plan is to "figure it out later." Gotta love hindsight.

Isolation, The Excuse Between You And True Potential

Being isolated means not having the chance to engage or be challenged by community. A friend, who is a professional DJ performs on most evenings, weekends and holidays, discussed with me how it always amazes him how people perceive his career as extremely social and inspired. He feels most of the time, he is at the front of the room, disconnected from the audience, and with no friends or family around. His observation is that being isolated is as much about routine and state of mind, as it is about specifics. It could be said that isolation can evoke feelings of loneliness, sadness, frustration, being left out, hopelessness; all of which limit our belief in our possibilities or confidence.[7] However, I believe that this is secondary, an outcome and not the cause, nor the problem. I view isolation as the barrier causing disconnect in personal and professional evolution. Anyone who feels isolated, in my humble assessment, is feeling that due to a lack of inspiration and influence from social and professional surroundings. But mostly, it's due to a well-justified collection of? You guessed it, excuses.

Poor Me

It has come to my attention that, for me, the biggest inhibitor is my ability to restrict myself by making excuses based on my *isolation*. The focus always turns back to the "if only" dialogue, focusing on the have-nots; building a wall of why I cannot actualize an opportunity and dream. The excuses of how isolation had wrapped my hands in chains were so easily justified in my mind, that I was not able to begin to construct a way around those very *real* and *unavoidable* restrictions. For example, working on a yacht with my daily routine, I blamed the lack of higher ups that I could look to for inspiration or challenge and was frustrated by it. I zeroed in on it being the fault of my circumstances that I have not moved more closely to my next level of achievement. I told myself that once I left that career, and was around people who share similar passions, then I would be able to move like wildfire towards building my dreams. Part of this excuse was created due to the lack of clearly defined goals, and a plan.

---

[7] Cornwell, E.Y. & Waite, L.J. (2009). Social Disconnectedness, Perceived Isolation, and Health among Older Adults. Journal of Health and Social Behavior, 50.1, 31–48, Retrieved from: https://www.ncbi. nlm.nih.gov/pmc/articles/PMC2756979/

Which, of course, I could justify by my supposed lack of inspiration due to isolation and access. POOR ME, no?!

To add to the mix is that little inner analyst reviewing the activities of peers, those who seem to have it all together, who's online posts are all about achievements, children, new homes, and vacations - ones who have figured it out on the first shot. We all do it, you know what I mean, compare ourselves to all the others who *didn't make the same mistakes;* who are *so lucky.*

To explain my perceived lack of "success" resorted to labeling myself a "late bloomer," how bad is that? Like there is a defined structure on my life's process, and somehow, I am late to get there. Comparison is the ultimate accomplice to excuses. In this case, it pacifies the voice in my head - justifying my reasons for coming up short and turning negative self-talk into a soothing voice of logic.

Until recently, there were no confrontations with that voice. But, once I could acknowledge my self-generated BS (excuses), the walls of my excuses began to look feeble. So, I slowly started to face the facts and call it what it was - excuses, soon all I was left with was a need for action steps. Seems simple? Seems too simple! The hardest part was admitting how scared, and complacent I had been. And so, began the daily actions to eliminate the wall (which is repeated and failed daily). Step 1 - **No Comparison**, Step 2 - **Create a plan**, Step 3 - **Repeat Steps 1 and 2.** Go on "late bloomer" get your bloom on.

It's Not All About Positive Thinking

"Here is my wish and here is why I cannot have it." ~ Barbara Sher

In a fantastic, (and funny) TEDx presentation[8], Barbara Sher suggests that we need to divulge our complaints, throw our excuses in the front of our peers, complain, and seek help. From her talk, I realized perhaps spending our time focusing on positive affirmations, trying to combat the voices of doubt may not be the right method. Perhaps what is required is identifying the complaint (i.e. excuse / comparison).

---

[8]Sher, B (2016, Dec 22). TEDx Talks: TED. (2016, Dec. 22). Barbara Sher. Isolation is the dream-killer, not your attitude [Youtube video file]. Retrieved from https://www.youtube.com/watch?v=H2rG-4Dg6xyI

Sure, repeating a mantra of self-adoration MAY make you believe in yourself enough to change everything. But repeating "I Am" (insert self-encouraging affirmation here) is, at best, only one ingredient in a self-development cocktail. All the repeated claims in the world would not alone provide the influence and community I sought. Something had to give, waiting for it to drop out of the sky onto my lack of access lap was not cutting it. I started to identify the obstacles, not to complain about them, but to expose them (thanks, Tedtalk / Barb).

I looked at my complaints:

"No mentor," "No opportunity to meet like-minded people," "Too far away," "No one to inspire me." I began to find routes to bridge the *have nots* with *possibilities to have*. Luckily for me, we live in a technological era, and connecting with like-minded peers is just a click away. So much for my isolation excuse. The wonder of it all.

Get Connected

"A tribe is a group of people connected to one another, connected to a leader, and connected to an idea. For millions of years, human beings have been part of one tribe or another. A group needs only two things to be a tribe: a shared interest and a way to communicate."
~ Seth Godin, Tribes: We Need You to Lead Us

During the time of my excuse cleanse, I developed techniques to build ladders over the walls of my isolation. I enrolled in online university courses, I spent my holidays in workshops and pieces of training, but I lacked consistency. I lacked a community.

Slowly, while on a quest of self-improvement by exposing the excuses I had created, I began to uncover what I truly needed. For me, the solution became obvious, I needed a **tribe**; how to get it was a bit trickier, but I began by looking outside my excuse of the job and geographical restrictions. I looked to online groups I could create a dynamic community with; ones that gave me accountability and measurable goals (which is how I found my way into this book). Once I stopped looking at my circumstances as something that I would have to *wait out* until the timing and situation were more favorable, I saw more opportunities to build my tribe. To do this, I started to ask:

How is isolation limiting to opportunities for:

- Growth

- Change

- Personal and professional development

- Inspiration

- Motivation

- Challenge

What can I do to eliminate the limitations?

- Find an online personal development network (many free social media ones exist)

- Seek to modify the routine just slightly (I started taking my morning coffee break outside to find a minute of quiet reflection, or reading a few pages of a book before getting out of bed)

- Online or community courses (Groupon offers some great discounts, or other companies offer free intro classes)

- Reading - especially inspiring stories

- Watching TED Talks, and even listening to music has helped me build belief and find inspiration

- To find motivation, I have reached out to a friend to have an accountability partner- even if it is to commit to small tasks such as reading a book

- Setting new small goals to break the barriers

Start small, with the things you know you can keep up daily, not a list of twenty new tasks. Setting small achievable tasks builds confidence - setting goals we cannot realistically make straight out of the gate, can undermine our belief in ourselves. For example, if one of your excuses is a lack of connection with a healthy network, don't start by signing up for a marathon. You've all heard it before: *"set small achievable goals."* If we don't achieve the goals we set for ourselves, we will fall deeper into self-doubt. And as obvious as it seems, don't spend your time and energy trying to build your confidence in places you are the least self-assured! Building belief in ourselves enables us to build confidence. We can call on these achievements when the comparison voice in our head starts to tell us we aren't doing well.

Eliminate The Routine. Omit The Excuse.

By allowing myself to blame my circumstances, I had given up the idea that I could change or improve my opportunities. There was this wall of reasons why - so called facts for my unachieved-ness. But this is the kicker, right? How could I possibly find a way out of the thing that appears SO valid?

Recognizing the potential that there would NEVER be a time without some form of isolation, empowered the idea of the possibility of starting NOW.

As Ky-Lee Hanson (the ambitious creator of this book) points out, life is a balance of sacrifice and effort, finding opportunity in our limitations is what makes the exceptional standout in a sea (sailor pun intended) of those who choose to use their excuses to remain with the masses.

I exposed the excuse such as *I have no community.* I uncovered this as a problem, and thus just needed to find a solution. Ha! What did it take to address the problem of not having a community? Pretty obvious - get a community. I signed up for various co-operative projects and started to create an online community. When the routine switched, the excuse evaporated. Now, this doesn't mean that I was instantly faced with exceptional opportunities breaking down my door, but they started to pop up like spring flowers waiting to bloom. By taking action, creating possibilities BECAME the perfect situation. And realizing that, I alone, had the power to shift this around by simply DOING something small, was like putting on sexy heels with a pair of jeans. The jeans looked ok in flats, and they were indeed serving their basic function. But, by putting on a pair of heels, there is a minor, but impactful change - there's new confidence, new potential, and because of that little bit of added height in your stance, you can see a little further.

"You're off to Great Places! Today is your day! Your mountain is waiting, So... get on your way!" ~ Dr. Seuss, Oh, The Places You'll Go!

Chapter 8

I Forgot That I Am Good Enough

by Cindi Melkerson

". . . not all wisdom is attained through winning a University degree."
~ Eleanor Roosevelt

Cindi Melkerson

Lifestyle by Design | Creator | Owner | Risk Taker

Cindi Melkerson is leading her life from the frontlines. Her motivation is to live the best version of herself. She holds a belief that, "If it's going to be, it's up to me." She designs her lifestyle around family, church, cooking, travel, fitness, friends, and her home-based business.

For years, Cindi lived from the mindset of fear. It wasn't until she entered the world of network marketing that she discovered a new and improved version of herself. Through her business and personal motivation for self-improvement, she realized the only way to live a meaningful life is to get clear on what you want it to look like. She jumped out of her comfort zone, adopting daily disciplines that have helped her develop a new found sense of self-worth.

Cindi lives by paying it forward. She believes there is no better gift than to give someone an opportunity to let go of what limits them. She enjoys the challenge of helping people dream bigger, and find solutions to their health and wealth problems. It is all possible with hard work.

For over 10 years, Cindi has worked in the fitness industry. She earned her Certified Personal Trainer certification and later studied corrective conditioning and functional movement.

Today, Cindi uses wellness and business coaching to open the door to a world of endless possibilities. She is having fun experiencing things she never thought possible. Her work is not complete, she is just getting started.

www.cynthiamelkerson.arbonne.com | www.linkedin.com/in/cindimelkerson
ig: cindimelkerson | fb: CindiMelkersonArbonneIndependentConsultant

Who is living a hurried life? After all, it does seem to be the norm today. Could it be that the *busier* we are, the more *significant* we feel? Is this feeling *authentic*, or is it a *distraction* that keeps us from a deeper internal feeling or desire?

Can we bear the pain of exploring what our greater purpose is? Have we lost the ability to *dream* of the possibilities of *feeling* joy, connection, and purpose? Could we secretly be listening to old stories and circumstances that keep playing like an old movie in our head? Our thoughts, perceptions, values, conclusions, and behaviors are the result of our past experiences in life and are stored deep in our subconscious mind. What we think about expands, and over time we begin to live this story as the truth. I lived my life based on the story that I was not good enough because I did not have a University degree. My reality of life was limited based on the beliefs of who I was and what I had not achieved.

Do Not Give Your Past The Power To Define Your Future

This was my life for many years. I was restless, as I carried a deep dark secret. My self-worth was coming in quite low on the scale. Here's my story: I lost my dad at 10 years old. I remember the day he died, perfectly. At that time, I was taking baton lessons, and had just finished practicing outside and came in all excited to share the news of my successful practice with my mom. She hugged me and then broke the news that my dad had slipped into a coma overnight. He had been battling cancer for months, and he was resting at home. I really didn't understand that he was going to die. Like a knife in my 10-year-old heart, all I could think about was that I did not say goodnight to him the night before. *How could this be? How could I forgive myself?* I was never going to have another word with him, *how selfish of me.* Mom brought me up to see him, and we all sat together staring at him struggling to breathe and then, his last breath. I'll never forget that sound, EVER. My aunt said, "C'mon honey, let's go downstairs and get a donut." Talk about associating pain with sweets. It's something I faced for years and years. I didn't realize this brain association of pain to sweets until I was well in my forties.

I remember my mom taking four of the seven kids on vacations twice a year. The three oldest siblings were in their late 20's and early 30's. I was the youngest of seven, and I suppose this was my mom's way of keeping us united. While in high school, mom invested money in a large ladies clothing store. Dori's Plus Size was doing well, so store number two opened. This is where it went downhill. Overextended and no way out but to close the shops, left us with little money - and bills galore. I was 17 years old, still too immature to understand fully, but I knew in my gut, it was bad. I can only imagine what mom was feeling and experiencing. Next came the selling of the house I grew up in and moving to an apartment. Through all of this came my realization that the *normal* college route would not be in my future. I never even thought about attending university because it cost money, and I didn't know where it was going to come from. I had settled in my mind that getting a job was going to be my reality. I think this is where the numbing and suppressing began.

My internal world was struggling with a feeling of low self-worth! When my friends would be home for holidays, I felt out of place. They would be talking about experiences at school, while I was already immersed in the 9-5 world, working a J-O-B, making a wage, and getting by day to day. I felt small and ashamed. I began to feel isolated, alone, and insignificant. Here's that story - you will never be a nurse, a writer or business person. My childhood circumstances filled me with confusion and a lack of significance. Over the years, my outside world looked pretty good. I made it look good by keeping myself *busy*! I was making a decent salary as an administrative assistant, I bought my first car, and was engaged to my high school sweetheart, Jon.

A few years after we were married and moved into our first home, I toiled in making some extra money. I discovered I was pretty good at sewing drapery for ourselves and a few others, and I also began selling dried flower arrangements and holiday crafts that I created. These things made me feel important. I always dreamed of owning a flower shop but never thought it could be possible because I knew nothing about owning a business. My heart was HEAVY. I'd make extra money for a while until I hit a roadblock, and then I would quit. I would stuff any idea deep down as my perception of not being good enough or successful paralyzed me. I continued to compare, judge and make myself small. There was that story again, "C'mon honey let's go get a donut." I ate lots of sweets to soothe my soul quickly. I felt alone, and it was scary.

That Was Me Then; This Is Me Now - Something Changed

Danielle LaPorte says that, *"Your life unfolds in proportion to your courage."* Sometimes, all it takes is listening to a compliment and sitting and pondering on it. This was the shift for me. My unfolding began with an acquaintance saying, "Hey, you would make a great personal trainer. Have you ever thought about getting certified?" Wait, was I just recognized for MY training ability? Oh, that felt amazing.

Sitting with a compliment, feeling the outcome as you allow it to expand in your mind is a good place to start. *Could becoming a personal trainer give me meaning? Could the process of becoming certified satisfy the education experience that I desired?* This would allow me to hold a position of significance with more income potential. Applying an action to a thought is the first step. Technology was changing, and I realized that the internet was a great resource that I could utilize to help support the idea of a personal training certification. Inquire and educate yourself on the process.

Allow fears to enter briefly, it's normal, but play with the visual of already achieving your unfolding. Develop your thoughts and beliefs as they create your reality.

I began to feel excitement at the thought of studying to become a personal trainer. *Wow, I would finally hold a position of significance. Could this be possible? I hadn't studied anything for over 20 years. What if I failed the test? Then what?* Oh, I was scared.

It Is Possible

I registered with the National Strength and Conditioning Association to become a Certified Personal Trainer. There was another certification available but you needed to have a University Degree, so I went for what was available to me. I didn't let this reminder of not having a university degree bankrupt me this time. I conquered and chose a new me. I ordered my materials and arranged for tutoring from the gym manager. Throughout my studies, the human body amazed me, particularly the body in movement and how it all works together. In a few months' time, I prepared myself and felt ready to go for it. I registered to take my test in Florida. Each little step of courage gave me a bit more faith that I could achieve more. Yay, I passed my test!

Replace Old Thoughts With New Ones - Dream Big

We physically change day by day. So why do we cling on to old ways and thoughts? These thoughts, fears, and deceptions leave our souls in constant struggle. You cannot fully experience and enjoy your true authentic self if you are always looking in the rearview mirror.

"The ruined life is not to be enhanced but replaced - we must simply lose our life, that ruined life about which most people complain so much anyway." ~ Dallas Willard

How do we begin to change our thoughts, replace them with new ones and begin to dream again? First, it's a decision that we no longer want to give power to our *old way* of thinking. Next, look forward and begin to play with your secret dream. You know, the one that you freely thought about when you were young. It's all possible when we let go of our limiting beliefs, and take the elevator down from our head to our heart. I was dreaming about creating a life of significance, holding a position that would contribute to our family's wealth. I wanted our family to have a choice, to give back and make a difference in the world. I knew this wasn't going to happen by solely working as a personal trainer. Although, I absolutely loved helping people achieve their fitness goals; I was trading time for money. I only received an income for the hours I worked. I couldn't control people canceling their sessions for what was happening in their lives. I knew physically and mentally that I was not going to keep this career long-term. I kept thinking about what could I do to create this in our lives?

Over time, an opportunity found me. I was asked to look at a business with a health and wellness company. This opportunity was in the network marketing industry. I knew nothing about sales, yet alone the industry. What I did know was that I was a product person, and knew lots about nutrition. This was a business for **everyone**, so my education no longer limited me. This business would be my vehicle to achieving my dream.

"If someone offers you an amazing opportunity and you are not sure you can do it, say yes - then learn how to do it later." - Sir Richard Branson

If It's Gonna Be, It's Up To Me

I chose to become a professional network marketer. I jumped right in. I registered as an Independent Consultant, and I received my very own website. This is the place I would direct my customers to shop. I followed the company's system, plugged into company sponsored business trainings, and created a list of people I knew, with whom I could begin to share my business. I was eager to start and started reading about other successful individuals in the industry. I realized they were no different than I was. As a matter of fact, we had quite a bit in common. We shared the vision of taking control and setting out to better improve our lives.

Like starting anything new, I had fears about what my family would think, and wondered if would they support me. I was committed to the process because I had been successful at starting my own personal training business so why couldn't I apply the same work ethic and learn to build a health and wellness business.

I launched my business by inviting people to my home to learn about this exciting journey I was embarking on. I was super proud and excited, but something happened that paralyzed me. A very good friend didn't want to attend because she wasn't looking for any new products because she was happy with what she had. I hung up the phone in tears. The first of thousands of rejections I would experience. My thoughts in my head were - *How could she not come to support me? I supported every little thing she started such as her cooking classes and her spice bottles. Yikes, what had I gotten myself into?* My thoughts were falling back to my old ways of thinking.

Everything in life will have its challenges. It's what you do with the challenges that make you feel a certain way. I had to get to work on myself and develop a rock solid, confident mindset. This is the most wonderful gift I have ever given myself. The gift of personal development. I am a committed, lifelong, personal development junkie because there is so much more to discover about myself. It is the personal care and maintenance of myself that allows me the capability of troubleshooting when things become stagnant in my business and life. By reading 10 pages per day of personal development books, I have developed a mindset that not only serves me, but I am better to serve the world. I have gained confidence. Some of my favorites are *Think and Grow Rich*, *The Slight Edge*, *The Flip Flop CEO*, *The 12 Pillars*, and *The Gift*.

Examine What You Tolerate

I tolerated a small mindset for years, and I truly forgot that "I am good enough." I was my own prisoner stuck in a loop of gremlins chattering in my head. I shut down the gremlins by shutting out the *world* of what I perceived people thought of me, to my reality of what I thought about me. Who was I to determine what others thought of me? How selfish of me to live my life through what I *thought* to be true. Faith, courage and personal development allowed me to feel and see this. No longer was I going to tolerate that everyone else was smarter than I was.

There is a big delicious world out there waiting to welcome you! What are you willing to shut-down in your life that you might be tolerating? It's time to elevate your life. Explore how you want to feel, allow your passions to surface, sit with these feelings and enjoy them for some time. Technology has evolved significantly, and there is a resource for just about every thought. You may need to find a professional coach to help you through this. There are millions out there waiting to serve you. One step in front of the other creates your reality. It's all the little things that you do daily that determine what you tolerate in your life.

Where Will You Be In 5 Years If You Continue Doing What You Are Doing?

The most important thing about you is not the thing you achieve; it is the person you become. I have not yet arrived at what I am going to achieve in my life, as I am still becoming and discovering that person who is good enough! I have developed the mindset of paying it forward to make a difference in this world. One opportunity leads to another. I see it, I feel it, I am presently living it; I'm just not done!

Endless opportunities are available to each one of us, and it is never too late to get started or change your direction. You can reprogram your mind and replace your limiting beliefs with very specific, exciting, and positive thoughts which then become your new beliefs. It's your time to create that different picture in your mind, see it, and feel from the end as if it is already true. There is only one of you in this world. You are GOOD ENOUGH to set the world on fire.

"I see life as one long University education that I never had." ~ Sir Richard Branson

Chapter 9

Say Yes To Your Sweet Spot

by Lisa Gartly

"I think we each have a personal sweet spot... It's the state of mind in which we experience the most joy and satisfaction in being ourselves and from that place of pleasure and joy in being ourselves, energy arises to flow out into our day bringing with it the depth and resonance of our own beingness, bringing with it blessings."
~ David Spangler

Lisa Gartly

Lisa is a full-time stay at home mom, who lives in Abbotsford, British Columbia, with her husband and her three beautiful daughters. Originally a prairie girl, she has learned to love the beauty of the west coast mountains and ocean. She is an avid runner and loves to thrift and decorate her home, making it a cozy, and inviting place for family and guests. Lisa loves people, and will choose relationships over tasks and to-do lists every time. You will often find her in a local coffee shop connecting with an old or new friend. For the past number of years, she has devoted her time and energy to caring for her family.

A few years ago, she started a network marketing business with It Works Global to further support her family by contributing to the monthly income. This latest venture has challenged a quiet, self-professed people pleaser and conflict avoider to step out of her comfort zone, put herself out there and face conflict and negativity from others, as well as from within. As a result, she is becoming a stronger, more genuine woman whose passions have been awakened. Her business has given her a means to express her passion to encourage and support women from all walks of life, to strive with her to be the best version of themselves. She has found her sweet spot!

www.gartly.itworks.com

Finding Your Sweet Spot

Do you remember being 18 and being willing to take any job available to earn money? Remember those summer jobs we hated?! I vividly remember cleaning bathrooms for two summers while in college as if it were yesterday. I didn't enjoy it! I tolerated it. It served a purpose, but I dreamed of one day doing something meaningful; something I would be passionate about. I have done several jobs over the years such as teacher's aide, retail, Starbucks barista, and volunteer mom's group leader. Each one has helped point me to a common theme. They have been a piece of a larger puzzle, pointing me to the burning desire I have today. More than anything, I desire to do something that I'm passionate about, something that maximizes my gifts and abilities, something I love! I call this my SWEET SPOT. It's doing what makes my heart sing. It's doing what makes me want to jump out of bed in the morning and give that day my everything. It's doing what comes naturally to me, and it just feels right.

The Reality We Live In

Living and working out of our sweet spot sounds so amazing, and yet the reality we live in is often so opposed to that. Negativity is everywhere, all around us! It bombards us daily. It threatens to limit us in every way. In fact, so many of us have allowed it to limit us for years. So if we can't escape it, what do we do about it? Even when we do everything in our power to be positive, that might not be enough because we aren't able to control others' approach to our outlook on life. Negativity can come from those we trust the most, from our families, from friends, teammates / co-workers, or customers, depending on what we do and where we work. It can even come from within, sneaking up on us, and sabotaging us by way of our mind, thoughts, and emotions. Some of us can avoid this pitfall more than others depending on our roles, jobs, interactions, personalities, but let's be honest, for many of us, negativity is a real challenge, and it has been for as far back as we can remember.

What is the reality you live in? Are you a full-time mom, an employee, a business owner, a retiree? I have been a stay at home mom for over twenty years with a variety of other part-time jobs. It's not that I lack motivation. My motivation for what I do - my *WHY* - is huge! It's to take care of my family, providing opportunities and options for my children, all while reaching out and helping others. Despite my best efforts to avoid negativity, I encounter and battle daily with its potential to take me out of the game. Here's what I've learned, often the hard way: EXPECT IT! It is unavoidable. It is a part of daily life. But, combat it by living and working out of your sweet spot. Focus your energy and time on doing what you are passionate about.

Have you found your sweet spot? It really is the ultimate antidote to negativity. It will help us push through the difficult, the hurtful, and the impossible. It will enable us to press down the negativity that surrounds us and get back up when we're pushed down. The key is to spend 90% of our time on what we do best, and 10% of our time on what we do well (there is no perfect job). What happens when we flip this around, spending only 10% of our time on what we do best? Discouragement and inner negativity grow, making us more susceptible to the negativity from outside sources. This inner and outer negativity becomes the *enemy* of our sweet spot! And a vicious cycle begins. See how vital it is? What is your story? I know that you have also probably done many jobs that you have simply tolerated, but what is your sweet spot? Uncover it and pair it with a proactive GAME PLAN, and you will have everything you need to be successful against the guaranteed negativity you will face. You will be unstoppable when you know your purpose, and are prepared! When we are unprepared, we react. We're always playing catch-up, never quite getting on top of the situation. Be prepared, proactive and preventative. It will give us confidence, and lead to positive, successful outcomes.

Having a Game Plan

Now that we've established that living and working in our sweet spot is key, let's look at creating a game plan so that we live proactively rather than letting life (pass us by and) happen TO us...We are most effective when we have a game plan set before us.

I believe there are six key ingredients to an effective game plan:

1. Belief

Believe in your sweet spot, in your passions, gifts, and calling. The world needs you, and all your uniqueness to do what you do best. Your belief must be stronger than the negativity that you will encounter. Your WHY must be rock solid and indestructible. You will get knocked down, but when your belief is unshakeable, you will get back up. Henry Ford once said, *"Whether you think you can, or you think you can't, you're right."* Even if no one else believes, you must. It will change everything!

2. Positive Mindset

If negativity is a given, then surround yourself with the opposite, positivity! Be purposeful about reading inspirational books, watching motivational videos and cultivating relationships with like-minded, positive dreamers, visionaries, passionate people. Go to events and seminars where you can be encouraged and built up. Isolating yourself and pulling away from others is a surefire breeding ground for the outer negativity to take hold and flood your thoughts. Don't forget to pay attention to your inner dialogue or self-talk! Sometimes, we don't even recognize the thoughts cycling through our mind, and the way they are negatively affecting our attitudes and actions. As soon as you find yourself caught in that vicious cycle, put an end to it, immediately replacing them with positive, life-giving thoughts. You must purposefully seek out the positive in every possible way, each and every day.

3. Don't Compare

The former President of the United States, Theodore Roosevelt, once said, *"Comparison is the thief of joy."* You are unique. Your sweet spot is unique. It is your personal journey. Don't compare yourself to someone else's timeline, successes, etc. As soon as you start comparing, you become discouraged, down, distracted from your purpose, ungrateful, and the negativity starts to win. Your *why*, or your motivation, has nothing to do with being better than others, achieving more, or making more money. Success means something different for each person. It looks different. Your *why* is centered around what drives you and is unique to you. Put your blinders on and stay focused. You do you! There's nothing better!

4. Gratitude

Practice gratitude every single day. It is hard to be negative when you are mindful and thankful for all the blessings in your life. List them from the smallest of blessings to the most obvious. Write them out. Keep a gratitude journal. It's amazing to look back now and then, and be reminded of all the blessings in your life. Tape them to your mirror! Share them with others. Speak constantly of your blessings, rather than your disappointments and hardships. There is always something to be thankful for. So much has been written lately, about happiness being connected to an attitude of thankfulness, and gratitude. An amazing book on the topic is *One Thousand Gifts* by Ann Voskamp. I found it so inspiring. As you practice gratitude, you will find your perspective transformed from the inside - out.

5. Self-Care

Seek balance in your life. Living and working in your sweet spot requires ensuring that you make time to take care of yourself and to rest. Taking regular breaks for self-care is healthy. And when you do, you fill your cup. Do whatever re-energizes, renews, and refreshes you. It is impossible for you to live, work, and give of yourself abundantly when you are running on empty. When your cup is empty, you are more susceptible to others' negativity, and to your negative thoughts and discouragement. Some practical and proven ways to fill your cup are getting adequate sleep, as well as exercising regularly. Equally important but often overlooked is taking "you time." When my children were little, I started taking Tuesday evenings off for myself to do something relaxing and renewing. I didn't let myself do essential tasks because then I returned home tired and worn out. It was incredible how two hours once a week made me a better and more effective wife, mom, and friend. Guy Winch refers to this as "emotional hygiene" in his excellent TED talk. Taking care of yourself is not selfish. It is one of the smartest things you can do to be the best you!

6. Clear, Unwavering Focus

Set your goals before you, and work passionately with perseverance and consistency. Develop a *WHY* statement. Why are you doing what you are doing? Write it down and revisit it often to remind yourself, especially on those difficult days. Be disciplined and unwavering in your focus. No matter what each day brings, be patient, keeping your goals in mind. It is helpful to have a list of your larger, long-term goals written out, as well as a daily list of attainable goals. Put your daily list in a spot where you will see it repeatedly throughout the day, so you can check things off as you accomplish them. Some of these goals will be accomplished quickly and painlessly, but many of them will take time and a lot of hard work. It also helps to share your goals with one or more people who will encourage you, and help hold you accountable. When our focus gets blurred, they can remind us of our goals. As you accomplish your goals, whether large or small, celebrate each one and then focus on staying in your sweet spot!

Signs of Being Stuck

Negativity is a given! It will come at you daily from outside sources. There will be people who doubt you and what you're doing. They will criticize how you're doing it. They will try and transfer their unbelief and lack of motivation, fear, and hurt to you. Acknowledge the negativity, but don't stay stuck in it! Know the signs of being stuck: lack of motivation, withdrawal from others, friends, teammates / fellow employees, events, etc. and not doing your daily tasks. If you find yourself to be stuck, fight against it with everything you have! You don't have to be a victim of the negativity around you or let it seep into your thoughts and mind. Get back to focusing on your sweet spot and following your daily game plan. When you are living, and working in your sweet spot, making a choice daily to follow your game plan, you may get knocked down; but you will have the inner strength to get back up again.

Accountability

Find an accountability partner you can confide in, and who can help keep you on the right track. This person should be like-minded and reliable. Sometimes you need to be able to vent and process, to let the negativity go and move forward. That's ok! Just make sure that this person can give you that little push to move forward when you need it so that you don't stay stuck.

Don't Give Up

Finding your sweet spot is a process. If you're like me, it began with your first job and has been a journey of discovery over time, from past to present. Know that you are not defined by your past. It is a part of what has led you to discover what your sweet spot is, and where you can live that out day to day. I know what my sweet spot is. I am passionate about helping others be the best version of themselves. Whatever I do, I want to be working with people in a meaningful way. I have found places to do that in increasing ways, and am continuing to look for new avenues and opportunities as I grow and change.

Throughout, I am constantly confronted with the negativity of others. I have had some family express outright disapproval, and others are completely silent and show no interest whatsoever in what I do. I have had friends ignore me, strangers criticize my enthusiasm and persistence, and teammates lose motivation and belief in themselves, and not have the courtesy, to be honest with me. I have also had my fears of inadequacy and failure. I have experienced success, and I have experienced significant losses and setbacks. I have had to struggle against negativity daily. And yet here I am! Resilient and having learned to expect it, and not be alarmed when it appears. I refuse to let it take hold. I refuse to let it win. I will ALWAYS get back up again, and get on with the business of living and working passionately from my SWEET SPOT! And it is my sincere hope that you will too!

Chapter 10

Trust The Path

by Katherine Debs

"Life isn't about waiting for the storm to pass, it's about learning to dance in the rain."
~ Vivian Greene

Katherine Debs

Katherine Debs has redefined the word 'normal.' Born in Lebanon in the mid-80s, it has taught her a thing or two about survival and living every moment of her life to the fullest. Her father being Lebanese, and her mother American gave her a chance to explore different sides of the world. She has since lived in Boston and Montreal. Katherine has a passion for helping others change their lives. She went to school for International Affairs hoping to one day become a philanthropist and give back to children all over the world. Her passion is also to empower people to lead healthier lifestyles.

For years, Katherine struggled with various health issues, but it wasn't until the age of nineteen that she experienced healing through holistic medicine. And she vowed to spread the word so that she could inspire others to live a healthier lifestyle. When the Arbonne opportunity was presented to her, it had everything she was looking for; a way to inspire people to make healthier choices, empowering men and women to take action and follow their dreams, and a way to give back to communities that are near and dear to her heart.

Today, she is filled with overflowing gratitude and love and shares it with those around her. She hopes that her three-year-old daughter will one day tag along on mommy's mission trips around the globe. She's a mother, a wife, an entrepreneur, an inspirational leader, a mentor, and an amazing cook. And she loves every role she plays. She currently resides in Boston with her husband and daughter.

www.katherinedebs.arbonne.com
fb: katherinedebs7

To those reading this, I hope you make the decision to not *settle* in life, I hope you choose to fight for what you believe in, and I hope you relentlessly and rebelliously chase your dreams. I grew up in Lebanon – 1980s civil war Lebanon. That alone was an exercise of character. Being born to a Lebanese father and an American mother, however, was another. Being the only girl among four brothers, in a patriarchal society, that too was a challenge; but these conditions offered me lessons for the future. Growing up in a society that had so many expectations of women – what one should look like, dress like, act like, and how to live every detail of life – it was all about *image* and what other people thought about you. I watched my friends all around me struggling to stand up for what they believed was right and fair. Experiencing this, I felt such heavy expectations of myself; but I knew I had a greater purpose.

I was blessed to have my amazing mother by my side. She taught me to stand up for what was right while remaining grounded and humble, despite wanting to break through the limitations that surrounded me. She fought my battles with me, and wanted to give me the best chance at success. Now that I, myself, am a mom to a beautiful little girl, I want to give her that same chance. The only way I can do that is by giving her the space to grow into her own greatness; lovingly guiding her, but letting her figure out her own journey. And she, in all her naivety, is teaching me exactly how to follow my bliss. I'm reminded of myself as a little girl; fearless and joyful, ready to take on the next adventure. My daughter takes it to a new level, never worrying about what anyone thinks, she's effortlessly following her intuition – knowing her emotions are an infallible guidance system.

While struggling for many years under other people's expectations, I was living as a victim; and I couldn't help but blame the conflict I encountered on the conditions of my circumstances. I didn't realize it at the time, but all the limitations I felt strained by were merely my own. The pressure I felt to push back was a result of the perception of lack I had built of the world around me. It took some digging but inevitably, I saw within me an abundance that transcended what I saw, or rather, what other people told me to see in my world. I had to clear the fog in my mind, and learn to fall in love with my soul, again – as do our children.

The journey to get here has been going for as long as I've lived (duh!) and it's been windy at times; but, persevering to stay true to that inner love despite the fog, despite the curves, is what taught me to be strong. I suffered with the image of my weight starting at about eight years old. I found comfort in food. It was my way of shutting the world out so that I didn't have to face the issues I was confronted with. I clearly recall a typical Sunday scene at my grandparents' house with my father's family. It was normal for the kids to sneak by the dining table picking at the snacks laid out before lunch. I remember the incessant commentary from the family telling me to stop picking at the snacks, because they wanted me to lose weight. Suddenly, my grandmother took me aside to her bedroom balcony and pointed to a neighbor in the building beside us, who was in her mid-twenties at the time. She said, "You see that girl across from us? A year ago, she was severely over-weight and nobody wanted to marry her. But she's lost all the weight now and the men are lining up for her hand in marriage."

Despite her traditional approach and what might seem as rude today, it was her way of looking out for me. She did want the best for me, even if that meant squeezing her concern through the frame of her mentality. Back inside, I joined my cousins by the snacks and before any chance of a comment, my grandmother pointed out to everyone, "No one nag over Katie's head. She'll lose weight on her own time." It took me years to reconnect with my truth, and having found it, I've come to understand that shedding every ounce of doubt towards my inner-self must come before I can shed any ounce of my outer-self. Limiting my happiness to a number on the scale beats the point of sharing unconditional love with those around me, especially if I haven't yet shared it with myself.

After this came my healthy lifestyle. Health has become an extension and a tool to perpetuate what I already know to be true inside. You could even call it a side effect of being joyful. Yes, being healthy makes one happy too; it's a positive feedback loop that just keeps giving! Nonetheless, health is only complete when it holistically includes the body, the mind, and the spirit.

Every Thought, A Step

I remember being a little girl sitting in bed praying for my life to change. I did not know at the time that I was using what some call "The Law of Attraction" – asking for what I wanted, and creating the path that would lead me there. Now, looking back I see it so clearly.

I had so many dreams and aspirations, and I pushed to make them all happen. I went to college to do big things, but despite my drive, at twenty-seven I found myself lost and unhappy. I was *comfortable* at my corporate job, despite the ever-increasing stress of the daily grind. For what is stress, but a beacon nudging you towards listening to your path? That suppressed feeling of longing will burst if you ignore it long enough. Like an innocent child not knowing how else to express its need to... express! And sure thing, my longing to be more, do more, see more, and want more, burst.

At the time, I was looking for a way to *own my own* life, to get out of the corporate world, and move on to becoming an entrepreneur – someone enthused with taking things to the next level despite the circumstances stating otherwise. I wanted the freedom and flexibility of a lifestyle not limited by market targets and trends. I *knew* something was out there, but I didn't see the opportunity right away. Almost as soon as I took my blinders off, I was presented with the opportunity that would alter the course of my entire life. I thank God that I was blessed with an open-mind and heart at the time because otherwise, I'm not sure where I'd be today.

And so, my network marketing career with Arbonne brings me here, and it's taught me to build a business and help others in more ways than I could ever have imagined.

I'm quite proud of the woman I've become. I've been a daughter, a sister, a wife, a mother, and a friend to people who share the same vision of abundance this business allows me to express. I've become an entrepreneur, a coach, a mentor, an inspirational speaker and I love every single minute of it all.

I was told this all along, and now I get it: *there is no struggle we face that we cannot overcome.* It is not about what happens to you, but how you respond to it.

Find Your Inner Strength

Not too long ago, I ran into some of my daughter's teachers after dropping her off at school. They were giggling at something when they saw Zelda, and I asked them,

"What's happened?"

They proceeded to explain,

"We love how independent she is. Just yesterday, one of her classmates told the teacher that Zelda pushed her."

I was not amused.

"And when one of us went up to ask Zelda what happened and if she indeed did push her. Zelda replied excitingly, 'Yes I did!'"

I was in disbelief.

"So, we asked her why she pushed her classmate, and Zelda confidently replied, 'because I asked her to move!' The girl was deliberately blocking her path and refused to move for Zelda. So, she gently pushed her out of the way."

I knew Zelda wouldn't bully and push someone out of the way, and so understood the teacher's pride in her decision to push. I'll make sure she knows that pushing isn't always the best choice, but also that her intention to stand in her truth and desire isn't wrong. She wasn't going to let someone else take away her freedom to move, and I'm glad she knows that. I always say my daughter is an entrepreneur in the making. Hopefully, with her study of language, she will manage her requests better, the next time someone stands in her way.

Sometimes, a push is all you need. Push the doubt aside, push the hate behind you, push the door open and take responsibility for your life. You are the captain of your ship, and we all know that waves must be pushed aside to keep moving forward.

Many of us wish we were dealt different cards in life. I used to feel that way too, but today I feel triumphant. The memories I've shared remind me of Maya Angelou's *Our Grandmothers*,

"I come as one, but stand as 10,000..."

So, had my ancestors, who passed on a dormant womb of unbridled self-expression. I have chosen to unravel what has only been a dream for the ten thousand before me. I have chosen to birth this expression of ceaseless love and hand it to my children, and them to theirs.

If you're reading this, and feel like you want things in your life to change, I'm here to tell you that you too can begin unraveling the depths of your inner freedom. I'm here to tell you that if you want to live a radically inspired life, then you have to dare to believe that who you are deep down inside is enough. You are so deserving of this life, and all the wonders it has to offer.

Don't be ashamed of where you came from, what you've been through, and what you have or haven't done; instead, look at your reflection in the mirror, look at your life, look at everything you've accomplished, and know that it is all so worth it. You are unique in your own special way, and the world is desperate to know your story and be inspired by it. So those scars you have, those scars that make up your story - they are your reminder every day that you have weathered the storm, and have come out triumphant and wiser on the other side.

So love yourself unconditionally, embrace your scars, and celebrate your story. The world needs you, all of you. You are enough!

Through all this, I hope that our paths unfold and intertwine and that we can all share a slice of this eternal journey together.

Section 3

Money Is Not A Limit

Featuring

Jennifer Jayde, Elaine McMillan, and Vickee Love

Opening commentary by Tania J Moraes-Vaz

In the previous section, we learned about how to transcend our perceived limitations, and rise above them in order to achieve our goals and dreams, so that we progress positively, rather than regress negatively.

Part of rising beyond our perceived limitations is also the mindset and thought process we harbor when it comes to our relationship with money. Far too many of us feel tied down and limited by our finances - be it with day to day responsibilities, leaving far too little room to spend money on any leisurely pleasures, or doing something we truly enjoy such as travel, starting our own business or being a part of a new joint venture, or sometimes, being unconsciously frivolous with our money. How do you feel about money when it comes up as a topic of discussion personally, with your partner / spouse, or a business partner, or any possible venture that you may consider undertaking? What are the emotions that come to surface when asked to think about your finances? What would your career and lifestyle involve if money were not an issue? If you could change the way you thought and felt about money in order to positively impact your life, would you?

Consider something John. C. Maxwell likes to call the "Abundance Mentality", vs. the "Scarcity Mentality."[9] To paraphrase, when one operates from a mindset of abundance, they truly believe that what they need will come to them and there is plenty for everyone; no matter the circumstances (or limitations) they encounter or perceive themselves to be in. Hence, all the opportunities they come across, any venture that they want to initiate or be a part of, flow seamlessly. Individuals who think from an abundance perspective are those who will push through their circumstances because they have a mindset to see *beyond* their current reality, and find a way to make something shift or happen for themselves. Conversely, when one operates from a scarcity mindset, they are more prone to staying with their limitations - feeling as though there isn't enough opportunity

[9]Maxwell, J.C. (2015, March 04) *John C. Maxwell: 6 Tips to Develop and Model an Abundance Mindset.* Retrieved from http://www.success.com/article/john-c-maxwell-6-tips-to-develop-and-model-an-abundance-mindset

for everyone. They hold onto their current reality, and are less prone to taking on new opportunities for fear of what may happen if it doesn't work out. They operate from a place of lack, and feel as though they never have enough resources for themselves. There was an article sent to me by Ky-Lee Hanson *(our tenacious, fierce, and amazing brain-child/creator of this book and series)* recently that discussed an utopian like city - Auroville, located in Southern India. [10] It was founded by Mirra Alfansa, who (like many of us) simply wanted to change the world, and create a long lasting positive impact. Auroville is protected by UNESCO, and is a prime example of how one can actually live the life they have envisioned. It is a city where every ideal that we hope to achieve and establish in today's dystopian society, has actually been achieved. They utilize the barter system instead of money, and are decades ahead in terms of sustainable, eco-friendly social and scientific infrastructure. It goes to show that money is simply one kind of organizational tool - a means to an end, that is widely used today. **Your potential knows no bounds, and is limitless; it all starts with your thought process**. It can be further honed and cultivated through daily actions that don't need to always involve money; so why *limit* yourself ?

This brings me to a quote by Robert Kiyosaki that has always stayed with me - *"Never say you cannot afford something. That is a poor man's attitude. Ask HOW to afford it."* Essentially, Kiyosaki too is talking about moving and reframing our thinking from the broke mindset to one of limitless potential and abundance. Overcoming your fiscal limitations, and reworking your relationship with money is all a matter of re-wording your thought process about money and any opportunity, and asking yourself the question - *What will I do to get to where I want to? HOW am I going to get to where I want to be in my life?* - This solution based thought process in turn affects the words you choose to speak out, which then manifests itself in your life one day at a time, by the action steps you take to live a life of abundance or lack thereof. A huge part of this relearning is to truly

---

[10]*Segal, S (2017, March 22). This City Really Exists Where People Live Without Politics, No Religion and No Money.* Retrieved from http://curiousmindmagazine.com/city-people-live-without-politics/

believe in yourself and your abilities, take a chance on yourself and use the opportunities you come across as a way to shift the course of your life towards a direction that resonates with you in the long run.

In this section, Jennifer teaches us how to attract financial abundance without chasing it, while Elaine guides us on how to overcome adversity, and really create the life we have dreamed of living by overcoming the doubters, and naysayers around us. Lastly, Vickee helps one realize that they do not have to feel limited socially, professionally, or financially as a woman, and how to kick the 3 B's (Broke, Burned Out, Bachelorette) to the curb. Remember, you have a right to thrive positively in all spheres of your life, and you do not need to look elsewhere to make it happen; *look within*. Tap into your personal energy and use it as your personal currency to manifest a life of abundance, and take back your power.

Chapter 11

Are You Being Money's Needy Girlfriend?
No wonder it keeps running away...

by Jennifer Jayde

*"Desire fuels our search for the life we prize. Our desire, if we will listen
to it, will save us from committing soul-suicide, the sacrifice of our
hearts on the altar of 'getting by'. The same old thing is not enough.
It will never be..."*
~ John Eldredge

Jennifer Jayde

Jennifer Jayde is an international speaker, author, and mentor that connects women from around the globe with their purpose and supports them in creating soul aligned businesses, knowing from experience that when your work ignites your soul - you will light up the world.

She comes from humble beginnings - a small town girl from Canada whose earliest memory was sharing a bedroom with her single mom in an old basement suite. At 22 years old, she became a 100% commission-based mortgage broker, and grew her business to generate over 6 figures in total annual sales.

By 26, she had a serious wake up call and realized her soul was pulling her to follow her childhood passion of photography. She left the mortgage industry and began her full time business, specializing in destination weddings. Jennifer became a top photographer in her region, garnering consecutive awards for her work.

She then felt the familiar "tap on the shoulder," and followed her passion once again. This time, in helping women around the world find their purpose and truly live limitlessly.

Within a few short months of starting her coaching business, she sold out her 1:1 coaching program, waitlisted her group program, and generated over a ¼ million in sales in her first year of business, helping women around the world discover their purpose and truly create their dream lives.

She now resides in sunny San Diego, but feels at home wherever there is sunshine and salty air...

www.jenniferjayde.com
ig: jenniferjayde_successcoach | fb: jenniferjaydedreambizcoach

I remember being 6 years old, my mom beginning to close the creaky door behind her to the little bedroom we shared after tucking me in one night. Before she could close it fully, I asked her in my little sleepy voice, "Mom, are we poor?"

She couldn't lie. "Yes," she said, "but it isn't for you to worry about..." Like hell I wasn't going to worry about it! I remember this as the defining moment where I decided I didn't want to be a burden to my hard working mom, and that I'd never rely on anyone else to provide for me. Anything I wanted in life, I would have to work hard and get for myself.

And there it was - my scarcity mindset and hustle mentality were born. It started with lemonade stands. It grew into making handmade greeting cards, and even employing a friend at daycare to help me make them. I graduated into having my own paper route.

Even though I realized at age 17, my dream was to become a photographer - I thought that would lead me to being a broke starving artist for the rest of my life, so I ignored my soul in favor of success. I entered, or rather, continued in the zone of working hard, hustling, and grinding, and became a 100% commission based finance lender in real estate by age 22.

I could say it was hard because I was a young woman trying to gain respect, trust, and business from an older male dominated industry. I could say it was hard because I was so young, but it was hard *because it wasn't my passion.* I sold my soul in exchange for what I thought would lead me to financial freedom.

How Do We Actually Become Free, When We're Chained To The Desk Of A Dream Killer?

I was in my mid-twenties now, having great money momentum from my painfully forced efforts. I could travel whenever I wanted, shop, I bought a house and a convertible. I got married and had my dream wedding at a castle...I had everything that society told me would make me feel happy and successful - but my soul was slowly dying inside. Around this time, as I was entering my quarter life crisis, *What have I done? Is this as good as it gets?*, I got a call that would literally drop me to my knees.

A young family member of mine was given 1 year to live. What had started out as abdominal pain, had turned out to be a deadly disease, and 10 months later when he was laid to rest, I finally woke up. I realized I couldn't pretend I had 60 years to live a life I'd actually love. I finally understood with every fiber of my being - I may not even be here next year, let alone 60 years from now. My biggest fear was no longer worrying about rent, bills, or not making enough money.

It was now having regrets on my death bed, over a life *never truly lived*. *"Who will cry when you die?"* - a Robin Sharma quote I heard repeating in the back of my head. I knew deeper than my fears of lack and scarcity over bills and rent rooted from childhood - I wanted to touch lives. Millions of lives! I realized that I'd rather take a massive pay cut and love what I do, than trade my life away by the hour, for ANY amount of money. This was when I began letting my heart and soul lead the way to my dreams - instead of my scarcity driven, fear based inner critic (ego) telling me to chase money.

And when I let go of chasing money, money started chasing *me*. More money than I'd ever known.

By trusting my soul this time around, I found myself creating a quarter million dollars in the first year alone of doing what lit me up from the inside out - coaching women on how to find their purpose and create their own dream business based on what ignites *their* soul.

How Did I Do This?

How did I go from $0 and clueless in the online business world, to creating the most income I'd ever known in less than 1 year - without chasing money?
I woke up to the fact that I had it all backwards.

That by chasing money - we're actually *chasing it away*. It's like I had become money's needy girlfriend; often thinking everything from -*Where are you? Why won't you return my calls?!* to, *I don't need you in order to be happy*, to, *wait a second, get back here – I need you. I'll change, I'll work harder, I promise!*

The First Thing I Did With This Realization, Was Start Investing In Myself - Immediately

I found someone to show me what a healthy money relationship actually was, and how to reprogram my subconscious mind ASAP to stop thinking and acting upon the scarcity mindset and hustle mentality I'd unknowingly harbored since I was a kid. I had to undo 25+ years of being addicted to money worries, and retrain it to be open to receiving, and feeling worthy of abundance, ease, and flow.

I also got the support I needed to create the life and business I actually *wanted*, rather than the one *I thought I was supposed to*; where money would be simply the result, the *bonus*, of me following my dreams, doing what I love, and lighting up the world in a way that lights me up.

Rather than being the focus of my creepy, needy girlfriend obsession, money became my *partner*. With this newly created healthy relationship, we were enabled to serve the world together in a massive and meaningful way.

When I reframed my thinking from, *how can I make more money?* to, *how can I serve? (in a way that EXCITES me!)* the more money I made, and the more freedom I had.

- Impact = Income

- Income = Resources for even further Impact + Increased Personal Freedom *to keep following your joy*

- And so, the beautiful soulmate relationship between myself, income and impact began! - *allowing more money to flow into my life than I ever dreamed possible for me.*

Even though it may feel counter-intuitive, we won't find true freedom until we find the courage to leap into the unknown, and finally listen to our soul's calling, and the impact we're called to make in our life. *This* is where we're met with abundance beyond our wildest dreams, in all forms. *To ignore this calling on your soul is to not only do a disservice to yourself, but to all those around you whose lives you were born to impact in a way that only you can.*

From Rocky Relationship to Soaring Soul Mates

What about you, Beauty? What has been in the driver's seat of your life's choices so far - fear of lack - *what's in it for me?*, or faith in what sets your soul on fire - *how can I serve joyfully?*

If you check in with your inner emotional guide right now, how would you rate your level of joy on a scale of 1-10 where your job or business is concerned?

Did you choose it for love or money?

Or maybe it started out as love, but you fell out a long time ago, and you've stayed because of the money... *You can be honest with me. I won't tell.*

Whether you're in a job that you don't love or have lost steam in your business, there are a few radical game changers you can begin right now, to shift from being money's needy girlfriend, and instead, becoming *success soulmates* with money.

Reprogramming Your Subconscious Mind for Success

If you grew up around any unhappy money relationships, the chances are that there are some weeds that need to be pulled from deep down within your subconscious belief system. Repetition is one of the most powerful ways to reprogram your subconscious mind. (This is one of the reasons why mantras and affirmations are popular - they actually work!). I'm going to show you how to take this to a much deeper, subconscious level:

Write a paragraph of your most highly desired daily feelings, core values, or ways of being that you desire to shift into. These could include your relationship with money. Here are some sentence examples:

- *I am open to receiving money now.*

- *Money flows to me easily and frequently.*

- *Money loves me, and I love money, and together we change lives.*

Then, use the voice recorder on your phone, and repeat your paragraph 8 times. This is a magic number of repetitions for your brain to actually allow these new thoughts to enter deeper into the subconscious as a newly accepted belief.

Every morning, while you are still in your dream-like state, hit the snooze button, pop your earbuds in, and listen to this every single morning, without fail.

Throughout your day, take notice as these new beliefs emerge into your reality. Slowly, and in small ways at first, then very swiftly gaining momentum. Express appreciation, even silently, and feel gratitude with every single occurrence, igniting the Universe to expand these experiences even further for you!
And watch your new reality unfold...

Gaining Soul Clarity

Take a moment and close your eyes. Clear out any thoughts and ask yourself the simple question, *If I were to receive the most meaningful thank you card in my life from someone, the type of note that would bring me to tears - what would they be thanking me for?*

Here's another one, *What would excite me so much to be doing, that I would not even care whether or not I was being paid to do it?* There is NO thinking allowed. Your soul will shoot out an answer immediately. Listen without judgment, and do not allow your head to dismantle it. You can do this in silence or use it as a journal exercise. The answer will likely come immediately within seconds. If for some reason, it doesn't, then keep asking yourself this daily until the answer comes. It will come as soon as you are quiet and open enough to listen.

And lastly, imagine you have more money and time than you'd ever be able to spend in a lifetime. In other words, money and time are limitless resources for you. Where in the world are you? Who are you with? What do you do for fun? How do you fuel your soul? What do you offer to the world, that is meaningful to you - not because you need the money, but because it feels really good to be doing?

Your Next Step

When you have even a foggy idea of what would excite your soul to be doing now, list 3 action steps that would start aligning you in the direction of it. For example, internet research, a coffee or Skype date with an existing professional, watching videos, taking a program, or hiring a coach. Beside each action step, write the DATE they will be completed on / before, and go directly to your schedule and create the time to do them. A dream is a goal that hasn't been written down - and as Marie Forleo says, *"What gets scheduled, gets done!"*

You have it in you to live the life of your ultimate desires. If you dream of being on Oprah - you can. If you dream of writing a best-selling book - you can. If you desire to make a million dollars a month - *you can.* These dreams, these seedlings of excitement, were planted in your soul for a reason. They're meant for you! They are a part of your soul's path.

You do not have to be able to see the HOW - the whole way there between today and your grandest vision. You can drive across town in the absolute dark, and you only need to see the 50 feet ahead of you that your headlights shine. The same goes with life. You will not see the whole path to your ultimate dreams all laid out before you. You will only see the path more clearly, once you continue to move forward by acting upon what needs to be done. Just take steps 1 and 2, and steps 3 and 4 will then be revealed to you, and so on. Move forward in faith, and trust that you are always taken care of by a force greater than you can even begin to imagine.

We are all born with a gift we were meant to share with the world. Half the fun is figuring out what that is. The blissful part is when you give it away.

In the giving away - you will be in the flow of receiving well beyond your wildest dreams. Money, time, compliments, opportunities, open doors, green lights…they're all waiting for you.

Instead Of Chasing, Get Into The Flow Of Receiving

Not sure where to start? How about the next time someone pays you a compliment, you allow it to land in your heart with a simple thank you. No deflection, nor shooting a compliment straight back. Or, why not try allowing your friend to pick up the tab next time they offer? And anytime you receive extra money off at the checkout till, or find a penny on the ground, or receive anything positive in general, shoot a silent 'thank you' out into the Universe.

I always say, I'm just a little Canadian girl from a small town and humble beginnings. No handouts, no head starts.

Today, I'm writing to you from a published book, talking about something that excites my soul - financial freedom coming from following your soul's lead. A quarter of a million dollars later, in just the first year of my Coaching + Speaking business alone, I now know this to be true.

And there's nothing about me that doesn't already exist within you.

If it's possible in the world...

If it's possible for me...

It's possible for you.

If you're ready to become soulmates with money and start creating a truly limitless life today, Beauty - have a peek at my website jenniferjayde.com. I have some free resources available for you to discover your own zone of genius to share with the world, overcome self-limiting thoughts and beliefs that will try and get in your way, and find clarity on what your exact next steps are from here.

This is the beginning of anything you want...

Chapter 12

Adversity & Your Empire

by Elaine McMillan

"In the middle of difficulty, lies opportunity." ~ Albert Einstein

Elaine McMillan

Elaine McMillan is an entrepreneur, who is a licensed aesthetician and spa owner of Beauty by Delivery Day Spa in the state of Oregon. Her day spa has won many awards since opening several years ago, which include being the #1-day spa in her small community. In addition to her spa business, Elaine is also has a mentoring and essential oil business. In this role, Elaine works with people who want to learn more about natural alternatives, as well as improving professionals' spa business. Working side by side with others and nurturing relationships is something Elaine fully supports. Through the spa, a lot of charity work takes place in the community, and Elaine also teaches others the importance of natural alternatives, such as essential oils.

Elaine is no stranger to building relationships with others. After having spent over 15 years as a manager and a top leader, customer service orientated businesses have become one of her top priorities. She works with her clients to share how to have success in their personal and professional life, and coaches learn and improve upon skills mastered.

www.myessentialmentor.com | www.beautybydeliverydayspa.com
ig: myessentialmentor | fb: myessentialmentor
t: essentialmentor | p: essentialmentor

I grew up in a tiny town; a small coastal community in Oregon. I knew for a long time growing up, that I had something different to offer. I had no idea at the time what that would be - my possibilities were endless. Things always seemed to work out for me, many times I had no idea why. As I got older and moved out of my parents' house at age seventeen, life picked up the pace. I got a full ride scholarship to go to college. I went, hardly had any income at this age. During that summer, I ended up working two jobs. I was not a lazy teen, I knew in order to live the life I wanted I must improve upon my skills somehow... It took me many years to find out what my strengths were, and how to overcome many of the hurdles in my life. I am going to tell you my story, this way you can see where I have come from and what I have been able to manifest with hardships, and hurdles. The road to success is so thrilling, yet you must have your big girl panties on. Every road to success begins with a beginning.

I went and worked hard in my twenties. I graduated college and moved to the city. I took my high school boyfriend in tow, and we began our new life in the city. Somehow, I ended up getting a management job [with no experience] at a call center. I knew that I had exaggerated in my interviews on the phone and in person. I had good people skills, all those years of working at a restaurant really groomed me. To this day, I always say people should be required to work in a restaurant. I had a great career for about a decade in sales and management. I loved helping people, and not having a boss breathing down my neck constantly. I also did not like the other side of the coin of having to fire and discipline people. These were the negatives I faced as I built an impressive resume.

One thing about me, is that I was outgoing, and I always got what I wanted. I loved thinking outside the box. By the time I was 29, I had decided that something needed to change. I had my first child at this time, and I learned quickly that working for others was not what I wanted to do anymore. I was not sure how I would become self-employed, but after my boss came in a few weeks earlier and yelled at my coworkers and me, I knew I was destined for more.

There were many "defining" moments for me in my twenties. I had the hustle, I had the grind, and I had learned some hard lessons.

By the time I went self-employed, I had a bit of experience under my belt, and knew I would need more. Some of the habits I had formed early on in my life, truly helped me in my quest for freedom. I wanted freedom of my time, and my pocketbook. I wanted to do more with my life, and by the time my second child was born, I realized that I had not done much that I thought was exceptional. In hindsight, I look back on now, and have decided this is NOT true. For some reason, I always had a challenge that seemed impossible to so many, and somehow, I pushed into getting it done. I often wonder why such tasks come my way, I have decided it's because I am one who can move a mountain.

My 30's, I say, is where I finally took control of my success, in my own hands. I had set a foundation of skills from the hustle of my 20's. I was able to take all the things that have happened to me to create a specific skill set. My skills were mostly networking, learning how to communicate effectively with others, and creating an empire out of my skills. I look it at like building a house; you need the foundation first. Then, you begin to add walls, windows, doors. Eventually, you will be able to get the perfect flooring and paint, and those finishing touches for a final product. I often thought about this as I began to build my success as an entrepreneur. At this time, I got a foot tattoo with my life motto "Difficulty Lies Opportunity." I see this as a daily reminder of how far I have come. It also serves as a reminder to myself when situations are not ideal, and I need to come up with a solution.

At age 30, my girlfriend Melissa, who owned a local salon, talked me into going to beauty school. It was something I had thought of for a while, but never did. The day my boss came in and yelled at the staff, I had told my coworker, "I will never work for anyone again." She looked panicked. She asked me, "What shall you do?". My response was one of pure honesty, "I do not know. But I know I will not do this." Little did I know this conversation was going to change my life very soon. Be careful what you ask for.

Within two weeks, I enrolled into beauty school. I continued to work a 32hr week, and then I had to commute 1.5 hours to school on the weekends. It was grueling. I also was pregnant with my son, but

I knew where there is a will, there is a way. I made it happen. It took me 18 months, and having a baby before I finished. During school, I had left that job - actually, I got fired. The first time I had ever been fired. But being fired was *liberating*, I qualified for unemployment, and just got back from an amazing Maui vacation.

I began working at Melissa's salon when one of my clients (who eventually became a great mentor of mine) told me that I needed to be in a high-end salon or spa. I had no idea how I would even do that, or when. There are not many opportunities in a small town, and I had moved back home several years earlier due to employment issues in the city. She offered me a small space in her building in town, and said I could work there…it was then that the idea came about to open a local day spa in my town. I had grown up in this little town, and we didn't have anything that was a high-end place to get beauty services. Soon, my husband and I figured out how to finance the project. I opened that spa with less than a 10k budget. Within two years, the spa was winning awards, and our books were slammed full. It took months to get in for new clients. I could work the spa business, and work with my kids at home.

Right before I opened the day spa, my friend from high school, Gabe, had come to me. He had these essential oils he absolutely loved. I had used oils in the past, but nothing like what he had introduced me to. I was hesitant to get started since I had been successful in network marketing opportunities in the past, and I knew how much work it was to "chase the dream." In the end, I ended up doing well. The essential oil business grew, and continues to grow, even today as I type this. I was so grateful for this opportunity, and I ended up replacing my income from the spa in about two years. I now manage over 500 accounts for this, and coach many leaders on how to do the business side of essential oils.

I began mentoring a lot of people. People were coming out of the woodwork to work with me. Then my newest area of income became a reality; I began to charge for my mentorship, and started to work with other oil educators who needed help, and coach salon and spa clients on how to improve business. I generated a huge following on social media, and to this day, I am impressed with the amount of tribe I have begun to build over time.

Currently, I work a couple of days at my spa, I work with my oils business, and I am mentoring many. I am living debt free, and I am raising my kids with my high school sweetheart. I often wonder how I got here. Then I was approached to co-author this book. I knew I had a story to tell. I knew I had something to offer, so I took the leap of faith and decided to do the project.

Many think my story is a dream come true with no adversity, and that it was easy for me to get to this level of independence; *to gain the freedom of time and finances.* Moreover, the time to raise kids, love my husband, and chase dreams. For a long time, I didn't think I could chase dreams anymore. But that is not true. This road was bumpy. There were times I wanted to throw in the towel. People thought I was insane at times for doing what I was doing. I always had that unshakeable belief in myself that I could do things others could not do. I was correct. But it was not easy. I have a few things I would like to outline about adversity in building your empire.

I was building my empire. I was chasing dreams and making them happen. In the middle of the adversity I faced, I continued. Adversity is a noun, mostly described as difficulties, misfortune, suffering, pain and trauma. So, as you can see, I had to become more than just a circus animal jumping through hoops. I learned some tips that helped me cope, and move forward with my goals.

Success Is NOT EASY

Many will say you have lost your mind. People will not always be supportive of your changes, especially if you're going against the "norm." Many people think you must work a 9 to 5 job, have kids, retire at 65, and call it good. I knew this was not the lifestyle I wanted. In my twenties, I feel like I sold out to having the life I wanted; it was not for me, nor would I attain it. I gained momentum in my 30's, and finally said, "If everyone else is doing it, SO CAN I."

As you go for your success, you will notice things change, people change, and so does your mindset. As you begin to make yourself into a powerhouse of success, you will find that many people do not have the same drive as you do. Many will find this intimidating and say that you're working too hard.

To be successful, you will lose friends, family, and for some, the tribe you love so much may disappear. The good news is you will find a new tribe to fill those spaces, who truly love you for who you are and believe in your goals. You will miss events as you hustle to make your dreams come true. All of a sudden, Friday nights are now spent working, instead of a night out with your friends. I have missed so many social events in the pursuit of my dreams. You cannot be everywhere at all times, so you will need to make sure that you know that ahead of time. This is where *prioritization* is a must when committing to success. I knew to work hard for a short time, in order to gain a long-term payoff.

What we do daily, shows the level of commitment to what we truly want for our goals.

You Can Do Anything You Set Your Mind To, You Just Do Not Know It Yet

Yes, this happens. It is a real situation you can find yourself in. Once you have truly committed to your project or business, there isn't much that will stop you. I often look back on the last 12 months, and I have accomplished so much. Some of these are accomplishments I never thought would happen. Some I never even imagined, were possible. I did things I never thought I would say, or do.

Stepping outside the comfort zone for me was intimidating. But I pushed through the fear - the fear of rejection, of not being liked, or feeling very uncomfortable. I love the advice, *"Do what you know you can handle, and take it up a notch."* Best advice ever. It is so simple, yet vital to your growth. That one notch above takes you in the correct direction; it will fuel your fire to live in the zone of being constantly pushed.

You are going to grow on this journey and commitment you have chosen. You will begin to see the world differently, and take on different tasks. You are going to find yourself along this process, and for some, we have been lost for so long, that we find we are much more than we ever imagined. You will shock yourself at times, and other times you will be disappointed in a hard lesson.

Make Yourself Better

It is an absolute must to make sure that you are taking care of yourself. It is enduring to know that you must push to keep yourself sane as you build your empire, and push your limits. A healthy diet, hydration, sleep, healthy relationships, exercise, personal development, and practicing wellness are all essential self-care elements.

Personal development is key when wanting to be a successful business woman. You will do the things that others will not do, which in turn, makes you unique. This approach alone will make you successful, if you can get your mindset in check. Personal development is a wonderful tool to improve your mindset, limiting beliefs, and negative thinking. You are your own worst enemy if your mindset is not wired for success. Some of the personal development I have pursued are listening to audiobooks for 20 minutes a day, attending conferences on subjects for my businesses, talking to other successful business women and taking courses. I love taking online courses. Some great courses are how to use social media, how to use video online and any type of challenge. I find that social media has a ton of other "self-employed gurus," and you can get a lot of training for free. Read books about your industry, as you want to learn as much as you can. I often visualize a sponge, soaking up water. Soaking up as much as I can, to be a better and stronger leader.

Visualization is also a strong tool. I often use this to imagine my next step. Close your eyes, and start letting your mind wander to your goals. If you seek a dream home, begin to see it in your mind. Want to be debt free? Imagine your credit cards being cut up or imagine sending the last payment for your car. Do this as much as you can. It works!

Make sure that you surround yourself with the best company. We are influenced greatly by our actions based on the 5 people we spend the most time with. Make sure you're spending time with successful people. This may be a hard lesson for some, but it has been the most rewarding for me.

The beliefs that we have set for ourselves can be changed at any time. Using the tools above will create a road map for your mind to work for you, not against you. You will find your thoughts begin to change for the better, and you will also become more compassionate. You have the power to do whatever it is that you want to do in this life. Take the time to improve yourself; you're the best investment you can ever make. The beliefs that we have set for ourselves can be changed at any time. Using the tools above will create a road map for your mind to work for you, not against you. You will find your thoughts begin to change for the better, you will also become more compassionate. You have the power to do whatever it is that you want to do in this life. Take the time to improve yourself, you're the best investment you can ever make.

Chapter 13

Broke, Burned Out, Bachelorette

by Vickee Love

"Everyone will suffer a disappointment or distraction. It's up to you to decide to let it drown you in misery or drive you to success."
~ Vickee Love

Vickee Love

It's been said, *"Vickee Love has a heart the size of Texas"* because it seemed since childhood, all she wanted to do was help people in any way she possibly could. She's never met a stranger. As an author, songwriter; plus life, relationship, and career coach; Vickee Love is considered a multi-faceted entrepreneur. Professionally, she spent 12 years in property management before realizing her desire to help people stemmed much further than assisting with shelter. She has motivated hundreds of people all across the world to release weight, gain health, love themselves, and find love. Vickee speaks on the importance of creating self-awareness, as well as genuine happiness from the inside out. You can currently find her on platforms or in intimate group sessions speaking life into women from all walks of life. You can hear her written works played from California to Jamaica, in the form of songs and jingles. Life's experiences had a unique way of revealing her purpose, and with such discovery, she pledges herself solely to the empowerment of others as she is led.

Vickee Love spends her time speaking vision into her clients' dreams, transforming them into a true vision, then producing an action plan to help them execute. Her studies in psychology, small business management, and Christian counseling has given her a keen insight to not only listen to an issue at hand but figure it out, and create a breakthrough route.

www.VickeeLove.com
ig: iamvickeelove | fb: VickeeLove

In America, women's liberation is a new phenomenon – within the last one hundred years to be exact. Prior to this time, women were seen as property - good for menial tasks and procreation. Women did not begin working outside of domestic fields until after the 1920s. Even today, women are setting new precedents by entering industries that are mostly occupied by men. In essence, women are still learning that they can succeed no matter the odds.

I've come across many women in my line of work who have goals and dreams. When asked why they have not pursued these passions, I am met with the same response - *I don't have money, I don't have time, I don't have support.* I call these the three B's: Broke, Burned out, and Bachelorette. Many women fall into one or more of these categories in one way or another. Of the women that fall into these categories, many see these challenges as debilitating. The three B's prevent them from moving forward, and many women see themselves as stagnant or even regressed. At one point or another in life I've been one, or ALL three of these at once.

We live in a world where if we chose to listen to the negativity that is so prevalent in society, we would believe that we could not progress any further than our restraints will allow. My goal is to teach women how to break societal constraints and achieve far more than they could ever fathom. I teach that the three B's can be overcome, and are not hindrances to reaching goals and dreams.

Broke

Not having money is not a good feeling. In fact, it's awful. Trust me, I know from experience. At one point in my life, I was a young mother who was jobless, homeless, and penniless. Nevertheless, the one thing I wasn't was hopeless. Statistics show that nearly 70% of Americans are living paycheck to paycheck. There are roughly 25 million middle-class families that have less than $5000 saved, and are literally a paycheck away from losing shelter, transportation, and the ability to buy food.[11] The chances are that if you are reading this,

---

[11]Markowicz, K (2016, September 27). *Why even half the middle class is living paycheck to paycheck?* Retrieved from http://nypost.com/2016/09/27/why-even-half-the-middle-class-is-living-paycheck-to-paycheck

you are one of the 25 million. You have bought into the lie that says that if you work hard in school and go to college, you can secure a high-paying job when you graduate. You may be surprised to learn that while that model worked in the '80s, most college graduates nowadays are unable to secure employment any easier or better than someone with a high school diploma. If you have a degree, you are most likely paying off student loans, and these payments usually prevent you from saving.

You are working to pay your bills, and that's all. You find that minor emergencies set you back astronomically. Your overdrawn bank account is a more frequent occurrence than you care to admit. I've been there, and the frequent payday advances I would get seemed to help, but in fact, they secretly pushed me into a hole. What if I told you that the reason you do not have money is most likely because of your job? Millionaires don't have jobs; they own businesses. They have created a system where their money is working for them. People who have jobs are working for money that is determined by someone else. If you are working a job, you are building wealth for someone else. You are making someone else's dreams come to life. Through you, someone else is reaching their goals.

Don't allow the mindset that not having anything will prevent you from succeeding and achieving. *Consider this, for example, the Biblical story of creation maintains that God spoke the earth into existence from nothingness. This is a great example of how powerful the words we speak can be. That is why in 1 Romans 4:17 (NIV), Paul teaches that we are to speak the things that are not as if they were.*[12] There is power in your words. I know that the first time you heard this was from a book / movie called, 'The Secret,' but in fact, this idea has been around long before the people who contributed to that book were ever born. You have been given the ability to speak things into existence, even if there is no evidence of those things near. To quote Joel Osteen, *"If you're always thinking thoughts of lack, not enough, and struggle, you're moving toward the wrong things."*

---

[12]The Holy Bible (2011). *1, Romans 4:17. The Holy Bible – New International Version.* Nashville, TN: HarperCollins Christian Publishing

Try waking up every morning and saying affirmations. Do not focus on what you don't have, but speak positive words. It's my personal belief that "I am" are two of the most powerful words in the world in reference to our lives. For instance, if you do not have money, don't say, *I am not broke.* By saying this, you have still spoken negative words. Instead say, *I am prosperous, or I have abundance.* Do this for every negative aspect of your life. Declare the good you desire over your life.

Broke doesn't always have to pertain to finances. Again, trust me, I know from experience. I've not only had my heart broken, but I've lived through the eyes of other people, never quite living up to what they wanted me to be. I've been spoken ill of, and talked down to by people I loved, looked up to, and respected. Thinking back on life, I was broken as a child. One of my earliest memories was being molested by a family friend on my birthday. I suppressed that memory for years. When I did remember it, the only thing that came to mind to help me forget it was to take every pill I could find in my mother's medicine cabinet. I was only 13. It took counseling to help repair me. Yet, till this day I still dislike my birthday. Fast forward a decade. I married my very best friend, and after years of trying to have children together, we experienced two ectopic pregnancies within months of each other. Can you imagine? Not to mention the way my marriage ended, which would leave any woman feeling LESS than a woman, but we'll discuss that another time. I *personally* know that character called *broken.* We've crossed paths many times. Likewise, many other women know broken. We generally tend to suffer from esteem issues because somewhere along the line we were made to feel inadequate. The restraint that we consider broke, pertains to our willpower, our esteem, our motivation, etc. The good news is, we do not have to stay in that state. Being broken leaves an opportunity to be mended. Speaking affirmations into every broken area of your life will play a significant role in your healing. One of my favorite things to tell new clients is to repeat, "I am healthy, and I am whole." Do this every day for thirty days every time you look in the mirror. Look at yourself in the eyes and declare that you are healthy and whole. Take notice of how you begin to feel each week and see if there is any change. Let me forewarn you; there will be.

Burned Out

Are you constantly fatigued? Do you find that even after a good night's sleep, you still wake up feeling exhausted? If so, you are probably experiencing burn out. Burnout is a mental overload which manifests itself physically. When you are emotionally and mentally worn down from constant worry, anxiety, or stress, you will experience burnout. Since burnout stems from your mind, no amount of rest will prove adequate to combat it. The only cure to burnout is to find a self-care regimen that will declutter your mind and allow it to relax.

Many women experience burnout because we are designed to be able to multi-task. This is a blessing and a curse. Women are psychologically able to do up to five tasks at one time, while their male counterparts usually can focus on one or two. This isn't to disparage men, but to point out how we differ. Multi-tasking can be a benefit when it comes to managing all the responsibilities that we have, but it can also be very detrimental. When we focus on all the problems that we have, we tend to get overwhelmed. If we constantly ponder on the things that we lack, we become worn down and drained.

Burnout causes people to no longer enjoy the activities that they once did. They begin to isolate themselves, and this can lead to depression. When a woman is going through a period of burnout, she will become exhausted by handling basic tasks necessary to live. This exhaustion leaves little energy for much else. To expect a woman to be productive during burnout is futile. Most women won't even realize that they are experiencing burnout. They will insist that they are just *tired*, that *there are just not enough hours in the day*, or that they are *stretched too thin*. These thoughts may be true, but they do not address the root issue, which is burnout.

Burnout is not the end, and it certainly doesn't mean that one cannot be productive. Burnout can be reversed with a healthy self-care regimen. There is a saying, *"An ounce of prevention is worth a pound of cure."* Ideally, you will want to implement a self-care regimen before you are in burnout stage. However, you may already be experiencing the symptoms, in which case, I recommend that you implement self-care immediately and for an entire day.

Schedule time where you can be alone and do something that you like. Then, carve out 10-15 minutes two or three times a day where you do absolutely nothing. Nothing! Literally, sit and completely relax, or meditate. This may be a challenge if you are one who stays busy constantly. No matter how difficult, stop everything that you are doing, and relax. After that, you may want to read a book, (if it is recreational), go for a walk (just for fun), listen to soothing music, or even write. If you enjoy a hobby, take some time to do it. There's nothing more important than your self-care. You cannot function properly if you allow yourself to become burned out. All of your responsibilities will suffer if you end up out of commission.

Sometimes a burnout can push you into bad thoughts, creating a cycle of negativity within your mindset. Things like, *I'm not doing all this work, I'll just burn the building down!... Why go to school? Escorting is easier!* or *I give up!* - I call it *stinking thinking*, and we have to choose to think good thoughts constantly. When I'm thinking negatively, I literally fight to think about something else, I just don't want to speak it or stay in the moment the thought existed in.

"When negative thoughts come, the key is to never verbalize them." ~ Joel Osteen

Your positive mindset is more important than the cares of life. You will get through your trials, you will progress, and your financial situation will turn around; you will get through the burnout if you maintain a positive outlook, and continue to focus forward.

Bouncing Back

Feeling burned out is rough. If you are already in the thick of burnout, prevention isn't going to do much for you. You need a 24-hour R.E.T.R.E.A.T. This is a formula that will reset your mind and rejuvenate your spirit.

R – Relax: Go to a place where you will not be disturbed. If you cannot afford a hotel room, ask family and friends to take your kids and / or pets for the evening. If you are married or dating, tell your spouse that you are not to be disturbed for any reason. For the next 24 hours, you will be relaxing.

E – Electronic Disconnect: Turn off all electronics (cell phones, computers, tv, radio, etc.) You are going on a complete disconnect. Do not allow anything into your mind. The goal is to dump, not to fill.

T – Treat: Have your favorite foods available to munch on. This is your day. Treat yourself with a glass of wine, some chocolate, etc.

R – Remember: Think about the times when you were stress-free. Allow your mind to visualize good times. Think of those memories.

E – Elevate: Put your feet up above your heart for at least 2 hours. This is easiest at the end of the night, perhaps while reading a book. Having your feet elevated will increase blood flow to your legs and will take the pressure off your lower body. It's amazing how relaxed you will feel after having your legs elevated.

A – Affirm: Look in the mirror often, and speak positive affirmations to yourself. The next 24 hours are about resetting your negative mind. Say kind words to yourself while gazing into your own eyes. Do this at least six times in the 24-hour period for no less than 15 minutes each time. Say phrases like, *I am beautiful, I am successful, I am whole,* and *I am healthy.* Two of my favorites are "You are more than enough." and, "Girl, you look good!" complete with snapping my fingers and duck lips. For some women, this is the most difficult but also the most freeing part. Allow yourself to feel whatever emotion that is stirred by doing this exercise. If you need to cry, then cry it out (I usually do). Say these affirmations until you believe them.

T – Table: Every one of us has issues and baggage that we carry with us, which is not beneficial to our health and wellness. At the end of your retreat, take some time to table the issues that are responsibilities, worries, concerns, etc. What I mean by this is to write down on little scraps of paper each concern, and spread them across a table face up. Then, prioritize the scraps of paper. Make a pile of those items that make you *happy,* one for the ones that make you *anxious,* a third pile for the matters that make you *mad,* and another for the issues that make you *sad*. The happy pile can be picked up and placed in your pocket. Those are the ones that are automatically good for you. For the other piles, separate them into two categories. One stack is for what you can forfeit, while the other is for those that you cannot. If you can live without it, if life will go on without you being involved in it, it can be forfeited. Pick up only the ones that you absolutely must have. You shouldn't be picking up much. For instance, if visiting relatives makes you anxious, although it may disappoint someone that you have decided not to show, it can be forfeited. If you've picked up anything up at all, inspect it and make sure it's solely yours. If it's yours, place it in another pocket. This pocket has now become your prayer pocket. Leave everything else on the table. Symbolically, when you leave your retreat space, you are not only leaving scraps of paper, you are leaving the burden of these concerns behind as well.

Bachelorette

The shame associated with being single nowadays has long faded into the past. It used to be that a woman who was not married by her thirties was considered an "old maid." This is mostly because the role of women has changed. The need for a man has dissipated into nothingness, as more women have become successful without a husband. The need for a man is not just for the financial portion either. Oh my! They even have goody bags with gadgets to replace even the feeling a man can give. Shh, that's another book. Don't get me wrong; the fact remains that all women desire and deserve companionship. As some women have done, I am simply saying that you should not let singleness prevent you from succeeding. For some single women, they see themselves as incomplete if they do not have a significant other.

I have friends who feel that they don't have the proper support to make it if they are not married. They think that to be taken seriously and have resources, a man must be involved. While it is easier to navigate the corporate and business arenas as a man, it is possible to do so if you are a single woman. You can be assertive, and you can succeed. Women are breaking down these *men-only* barriers every day. Guess what? You can too. Being single is not a plague. You are enough without a man. You will not be validated by your marital status, but by how much you know. *Your ability to speak with confidence does not come from having a man at home; it comes from within.*

Do not allow singleness to prevent you from moving into your goals. Some women are married, but feel that they do not have the support of their husbands. This can make one feel single. Imagine being married and feeling single! This would suck! Don't allow anything to hinder you. The people who are closest to you may not believe that you are going to succeed, and that's ok. Not everyone will jump on board to your vision. However, their disbelief is none of your business. You must stay focused on your goals; therefore, you have no time to worry about what someone thinks, and if married, that goes for your spouse as well. If they are standing in your way and trying to sabotage your endeavors, you can and should press on without their support.

Making Gains

Financially speaking, you do not have to stay broke. You have every resource available to you right now. You must identify it and pursue it. What are you good at doing? Do you have a talent or a hobby? What is your passion? If you are a good cook, have you considered ways that you can earn income by cooking? People are always looking for personal cooks, especially during the holidays. If you're near me, contact me because I'm hungry right now. Do you live near a military base? The young men and women living on base never receive a home cooked meal. Market your home cooked meals to them. If you aren't interested in cooking large quantities of food, grocery shopping, etc. Have you considered offering teaching classes? There are women who cannot cook, or who are not good cooks and would love to learn how to do so. Offer your services to teach them how to make delicious meals for their families. If you aren't interested in teaching, then perhaps you can write. Write a cookbook, take great pictures of your food, and sell it. This is just one example of how doing what you love can make you money. The same formula can be used for just about any skill that you have.

The steps are as follows:

Identify what you do well. It doesn't matter what it is. If you do it well, there is someone out there that can't do what you do.

Offer to do what you do well for others - Sell your skill. Because there are people who can't do what you do, they will be willing to pay you to do it.

Teach others to do what you do - Teach your talent. Offer classes that will help others learn what you do. People will pay for instruction.

Write about what you do - Write your wisdom. People want to learn. As the expert, you should want to share. You have wisdom around a subject; write it down.

Final Thoughts

There is the concern of what to do with the challenges that we must deal with on a regular basis, that do not keep us happy. What we do with those is vow that they will not stress us, and they will not hinder us. This is life. When this happens, reflect upon what I discussed earlier. You do not have to be broke. You have the power to be mended in more ways than one. Burnout can be avoided by having a healthy self-care regime. And if you get into your regime too late, as long as you're alive, you can recover by taking a personal R.E.T.R.E.A.T. The single life is not a cursed life. If you do remain single, understand that you are complete on your own, and should be goal setting & goal achieving. Find your passion, and capitalize on it. You have something within you that someone will pay for. They're waiting on you. And to everything else, know that the power of positive strategic thinking is real, and it can carry you places In your mind that the world will be forced to conform to if you stay consistent. Above all, remember that you will make it. If you are reading this, you will succeed. Break your personal restraints that are hindering your success, and leave the 3 B's in the Breeze.

Section 4

Fear Is Fuel, Not A Limit

Featuring

Rusiana T Mannarino, Angelia Mantis, Kelly Rolfe,
and Ky-Lee Hanson

Opening commentary by Ky-Lee Hanson

We have discovered so far that limitations come in many different forms, such as internal and external expectations, past experiences, and of course finances. Yet, the most undermined and least acknowledged limitation one can experience is fear. As the title suggests, fear can either fuel us, motivate us, and help us transcend our perceived limitations, or cripple us in our tracks, enabling us to stay static and stagnant, preventing us from achieving our all that we are. When channeled positively, fear can help us shift the course of our life, and stay in a continuous momentum towards what we desire. How does this shift occur, and what are its key ingredients? **A shift occurs in one's life when the desire and drive to achieve one's goals and dreams, is greater than any perceived limitations.** This is how we are able to push past the limitations we may experience. Some people have this motivation from a young age, and some lose it, some keep it, while some find it later in life. Motivation is something you create, it needs to become a habit. Let's go!

This weekend I lost a friend. A Canadian, not yet 40 years old, he passed away tragically while travelling. His name was Jesse Preston, and he touched so many lives. He was like no one else I have ever met. He had momentum; the contagious kind. He lived life to the fullest. Jesse didn't see things as limits, he tackled life as it came, and didn't sweat over the small stuff. He enjoyed life, and I mean really enjoyed it. Jesse was always out with people, the life of the party, and a good friend to everyone. I can't remember him having any issues with a person – instead, he treated everyone as a best friend, no matter if he had just met you or had known you his entire life. He stayed close with people; lots of people. He payed attention to what was going on in people's lives, and was present for the big moments, not only there, but involved. Jesse always caught photos of people having fun, and was in his share of adventure shots too. Always making people laugh, taking risks and performing daring acts. He loved to play music for a crowd, hit the beach to soak up some rays, and join a random drum circle. He ran his own business, planned events, and travelled. I think he lived his life purely for the happiness and adventures that life had to offer. He was motivated to live, and was motivated to show others how to live. He was very supportive of projects and businesses I wanted to work on. I remember my conversations with Jesse were different than those with others. He would actually listen, think, and take time to reply with something constructive. Jesse didn't second guess himself, and he didn't judge you. Things were possible. He would connect me to other like-minded people, and my life is richer because of that. He would be proactive and get things done. He would always be the first one to step up and offer to do what he could. He enjoyed being a part of things, it is what made him such a good friend. His life was busy too, he had a lot going on as well, but was always there for everyone and *often* in some sort of crazy party costume, with something new and exciting for us to try, or place to go, or person to meet. The weekend that he passed away, everyone had been sharing photos of Jesse on Facebook. What an adventure his life was! So many photos. So many places. So many amazing people from all walks of life. He brought people together, and it is happening beyond his lifetime as well. We have amazing memories to share, and are still inspired by Jesse to just get over the little things, take fear as fuel and get out there and live. The fear should never be greater than the reward of the experience.

"It is easier to fear, than it is to understand." ~ *Ky-Lee Hanson*

There is nothing thrilling, or rewarding about taking the "easy" road. Coming up, Rusiana helps us to realize our fears, and shows us what to do with them and use them to our benefit. Angelia shares with us her fearlessness through imperfect "when-life-happens" situations, and shows us that it is possible to to take control of your fears, and use them to bring about the change you need in your life. Kelly Rolfe helps us get into action and unleash our power by sharing with us strategies that we can utilize to manage our life effectively and act fearlessly! I, then end us with an understanding of our decision making process so we can move forward; and feel empowered to make a choice when a limit arises.

Sometimes, we act in certain ways that have become habit, we may even accept them as part of our personality; but WHY do we act in these specific ways? Why are we a stern no when it comes to certain activities or worried to try new things? Sometimes we may just not like it and that is fine, but sometimes we have underlying fear. Fear is normal and it is okay to have, if you do with it what you are meant to. It is easier for a person to fear something, than it is for them to take the time to understand the fear or problem. It is complicated to understand death, love, betrayal, heartache and pain. It is easier to avoid it, to fear it, to keep it at bay. As people, like most species on this planet, we are programmed with fight or flight. It is easier to choose flight. I see people take this route subconsciously and it becomes a way of life. As creatures of habit, we will keep doing as we have before. People refer to it as staying in a comfort zone, and what that means is you have built walls around you, and would rather stay where you are, than fight and break down those walls to see what else could be. Maybe your zone is perfect, but that is rarely the case. As humans, we are also programmed to want more. We *crave* more. If we take a look at a life like Jesse's that I mentioned above, he craved more happiness, more social interaction, more life experiences, more friends, more knowledge and more of the world. That is what he got because he was not afraid to go after it. He was not crippled by the "what could go wrong."

There Are Some People Who Fight, *Not* To Fight

In my business and life, I talk to many people. They find me easy to talk to, and I learn a lot about what is going on with them or to them. There are some people who no matter what you say, or how much you want to pursue something, will fight to shut down your ideas and change your mind. Remember, misery loves company. Some people cannot be happy for others. They are fearful and they wear it as a negative person. These people are stubborn, and unsure of themselves. They do not take the time to understand situations, it is easier for them to fear it. They may say they are trying to protect you and build up walls around you, *for* you. It is controlling. You just can't win with some people - have you heard that before? I believe there should be no win or lose in a discussion, that would be a debate. Debates do not belong within family and friends. People doubt and fear you even from afar without knowing you. Worry blinds their dreams and the dreams of others. You can be

146

fearful or you can take risks. You can turn your fear into courage. Instead of thinking of all the reasons as to why something won't work, think of what would happen if it does.

Chapter 14

No Fears, No Limits, No Excuses

by Rusiana T Mannarino

"The fears we don't face become our limits."
~ Robin Sharma

Rusiana T Mannarino

Rusiana broke up with stress in her first co-authored book *Dear Stress, I'm Breaking Up With You*, an Amazon bestseller for stress management in February 2017. Her challenging early years, life changes, new countries, and motherhood, have been a constant reminder that God is in control of her life. *Dear Limits, Get Out Of My Way* came in as an arrow to burst her bubble of fear and self-limitations.

Rusiana is a graduate of Tarumanagara University of Jakarta, Indonesia, who majored in marketing and business management. Although she spent ten years as a flight attendant, she always had the heart for the marketing world. When she was presented with a business opportunity three years ago, she embraced it with an open heart. Her hard work and genuine passion for helping others landed her a spot as the Top International Sponsoring Award Achiever for the Canadian market in 2015 with Arbonne International.

Besides reading, Rusiana is a travel addict, who also loves shopping, and organizing her messy home! She is fueled by the challenge of working around her children's schedule, women empowerment, and second change.

For most days, Rusiana's office is her dining table, but it doesn't stop her from running her global business successfully. She is exactly where she wants to be; home with her husband and her two young children, Francesco (9) and Carina (6). They live in Montreal, Canada.

"Put your heart, mind, and soul into even our smallest acts. This is the secret of success." ~ Swami Sivananda

rusiana@me.com | www.rusianatjiu.arbonne.com
fb: RusianaTMannarinoArbonne

Three years ago, when a business opportunity knocked on my door, I didn't open the door. Instead, I opened a window. Why? Because I thought it was too good to be true. However, I was curious, so I started the business anyway. I felt like a child looking into a "forbidden" playground where only successful people were allowed to play. Since I wasn't one, I stayed by the window pretending I was doing just fine. I felt like a fraud.

Despite the good result I was having, I knew I lacked something. I was doing the best I could but had difficulty moving forward. I was right; I didn't have a place in that playground. I better just stay by the window. It's fine. Then it hit me! *It's not true! I am not a fraud.* The window is not fine! I wanted to be on the playground and run around like crazy! I was just **afraid** to go in. I was full of fear. I **feared** what success might bring.

All the while I thought, playing small and being ordinary was enough. The reality is that playing small and being ordinary does not serve the world any better. I have a purpose, we all have a **purpose**, and we owe it to the world to fulfill it. **Fears limit us from growing to our fullest potential.** It prevents us from achieving the success we deserve in our life, and in our business. It's time to put on our big girl panties and let's run the playground!

Know Our Fears

Whether we realize it or not, we all have some fear; fear of success, fear of commitment, fear of the future, fear of rejection, fear of failure and much more. Some of us don't even know we have fears, and some of us are busy denying them.

Why Do We Need To Know Our Fears?

To win the battle! If we want to win, we need to know our opponent! As Sun Tzu once said, *"Know your enemy and know yourself and you can fight a hundred battles without disaster."* More often than not, we are our biggest enemy. Be brave and be honest as you answer this question: *what is your fear?*

How Do I Know If I Have Fears?

If you are ever feeling anxious, you may have a fear, or two. According to Dr. Karl Albrecht Ph.D., *"Fear is an anxious feeling caused by our anticipation of some imagined event or experience."*[13] When I was a child, I experienced some awful events that created stress in my adulthood. Even though I accepted what happened, and broke free from my past memories, I still developed some fears. The danger is no longer there, but I become anxious when I face similar situations. Take a moment to really think about any events or situations that may trigger this anxious feeling. I'm not talking about the feeling you feel when you're about to speak in public; it's more like a feeling that makes you want to close your eyes and disappear. Try to write it down on a piece of paper; it's a powerful act of freeing our mind from clutter.

Where Does Fear Come From?

Fears can come from anywhere. It can come from the environment and people around us, or because of any threats. As a child, I was told many false stories and mean words. To make sense of it, I developed certain fears to protect myself. At times, hiding behind my fears looked easier than building confidence and courage; I used fear as an excuse. I often pretend to be brave in front of my children, or that I am cool while doing a presentation, or that I am cool while speaking at a presentation, when in fact, I am shaking on the inside. Pretending can only bring us so far until we're tired, feel like a fraud, and have lost our self-confidence. Know the source of your fear and confront it.

What Does Fear Do?

"Fear kills more dreams than failure ever will." ~ Anonymous.

Fear kills dreams! Fear also paralyzes our ability to perform even a simple task. Even though certain fears have basic human survival

---

[13]Albrecht, K. Ph.D., (2012, March 22). *BrainSnacks*. Retrieved from https://www.psychologytoday.com/blog/brainsnacks/201203/the-only-5-fears-we-all-share

values, the vast majority of fears are just **excuses**. I made many excuses not to do what I should do to grow my business. The result: my business is not where I want it to be.

Have a moment to think about whether you are full of fear, or you are just not sure. Regardless, if you have even the slightest fear, get to know it. It may be the one thing that you need to change so that you can grow even more in your life.

The Reality Of My Fears

I am a product of a broken home. I grew up with a single mom who is an amazing woman with the biggest heart. She is my hero and my rock. However, I remember she was always working. As a child, I needed some connection to make me feel safe, but it was not available to me at that time. I grew up feeling lonely and lost. It was like looking out from a dark room into a lit window. I realized it years later that it was my way of coping with my fears. I created imaginary walls around me so I would not have to face what was out there. I was comfortable in my dark room. I thought I was safe. I didn't know that I was burying myself alive.

I had a mixed list of fears. When I was little, I was afraid of being eaten by the river monster! I also had a fear of intimacy because I was rejected too often. Over time, I learned that there is this thing called fear, and there is another called danger; both are not the same. Danger is real, and fear is not. Some of my fears were real dangers, and some were just in my head.

Fear is like our own oversized shadow that haunts us around. It will not kill us, but what will kill us slowly are the actions we take and the choices we make while running away from our fears.

When we run away from fears, there is no end to it. The only way to be free from fear is to face it. I have faced some of my fears and am still working on what is left. What is important is that I know my fears, and I have the tools to knock them down!

No Fears, No Limits, No Excuses

There are plenty of tools out there such as professional help, therapy, meditation, hypnosis, help from friends and family, and this book is one of them. Here are some victories from my journey, hopefully they can help you to win your battles too.

"You are more powerful than you know and they fear the day you discover it." ~ Unknown

Get To Know Our Self To Fit Out, Not To Fit In - Fear Of Rejection

Of course, we all know who we are, right? Well, not necessarily. We may know ourselves by all things factual - but, we may not know who we really are on the inside, and what we really want from our life. There are many ways to be in tune with our inner self; one of it is this exercise I learned when I was working as a flight attendant.

Take a piece of paper and write down the answer to this question: **what do you want people to say about you at your funeral?**

That question was like a wake-up call! Why do I care about what people will think of me when I am gone? While I am alive, maybe, not that I care, but yes, I will care a bit, but when I am dead? This made me think.

This was my answer: *At my funeral, I want people to think that I did my very best to live. (I also want them to cry a little bit because they will miss me).*

I used to fear what my friends would say about me behind my back, so I did things that they liked even though I didn't like it. I was slowly losing my sense of self, who I am, and felt less like me. I became unhappy, and I didn't know what I really liked or didn't like. I was not living my life for myself.

When I was working as a flight attendant, I needed to fit in, and I completely lost myself in the process. I remember spending all my days off entirely in the gym, because I feared I'd gain weight. I starved myself, and I took whatever pills the magazine advertised. I was still feeling lonely and unable to maintain any relationship. I might have looked okay on the outside, but I was miserable on the inside. I was lost trying to fit in, and I let fear control my life. Those were fears of rejection.

Let's go back to the question; do you have the answer yet? From now on, whatever you do, it should bring you one step closer to the answer. We are not living just to fit in; we need to FIT OUT. To fit out is to add value to something. We add value to our surroundings, our family, our society, the nation, the world, and humanity. We need to know what we can do best, what we like and dislike, so that we can do what we want to do, not what others want us to do. Knowing our **self** can be the greatest adventure of our life, so enjoy the journey!

"Everybody's got a past. The past doesn't equal the future unless you live there." ~ Tony Robbins

The Past Is A Memory And We Are Not In It Anymore - Fear Of Repeating The Past

As an adult, I realized that I am who I am today, partly because of what happened in the past. It shaped the way I think and behave as an adult. One way to better understand ourselves is to do some memory recalling. The goal is to make sense about what happened in the past that is affecting our life today. Let's pretend we're watching a movie about ourselves. Take out your old pictures or videos if you must, and look through it. Usually, it will trigger more memories. If you recall even the most insignificant unpleasant memory from the past, it is crucial to break free from it.

As a child, I experienced some forms of abuse that I do not wish upon anyone. As a mother, I can easily become super protective because I don't want my children to experience what I had experienced; but, I choose not to be a paranoid mother. I freak out from time to time, but I quickly calm myself down.

Before my marriage to my husband, I wasn't ovulating for 2 years. My doctor told me that I might not be able to have children of my own. There was nothing wrong with me. I just had too many stressors, and this was my body's way of reacting to them. Once I let go of my fear of not able to conceive, I got pregnant with my first baby, it was like a miracle!

What I want you to do is to look at your past, and dig out anything you may try to forget or deny. Those are normally a common fear trigger. Sometimes the fear is so minuscule; we don't even know

154

that we are afraid of it. It's buried so deep that we become comfortable with it. It prevents us from moving forward. It limits our potential to grow! Talk about your fear (no matter how big or small) with someone you trust. Remember it is the past, it won't repeat itself unless we allow it. Living in the past is like walking backward, we keep on missing the steps forward.

"Success is not final, failure is not fatal: it is the courage to continue that counts." ~ Winston Churchill

We Will Never Able To Please Everyone - Fear Of Failure

I was told that fear of failure is the master of fear because it kills many dreams, ideas, and desires even before they are born. I remember reading a passage saying that the graveyard is the richest place on earth. It's where great ideas, dreams, and desires are buried. Many had passed away without having the chance to fulfill their dreams, only because they were afraid of failure. This can't happen to us! The fact that you are holding this book proves that you want something better for yourself.

How many times have we put our dream on the back burner because we wanted to please others? We put ourselves second, third, fourth or last. We fear that we may fail to live up to others' expectations. The failure itself may not be so bad, but the fear of what others may think is what pertains to this failure and is mind numbing. Although we know that failure is a prerequisite for success, we can't escape the fear of disappointing the people around us. If this is something that you can relate to, let's crush this together. We're not a doormat; we are the doors!

I was taught that studying hard, excelling in school is the way to have a better life. So, I studied like crazy. I did well during my years of education. I graduated from university with good grades, and I thought that was it! I would be happy! I was, but it was just for a while; I quickly felt something was missing. My goal to study was not to be knowledgeable, but to prove to people that this child from a broken home can excel and be great as well. I was hard on myself because I tried to please others and I forgot to please myself. Failure is really the master of fear. It limits us from being truly happy! We can have all the success in the world, but if we are not focusing on our own happiness, there is no point to any of this.

"Do one thing every day that scares you." ~ Eleanor Roosevelt

I Will Fear No Evil For You Are With Me ~ Psalms 23:4

Imagine you have a time machine - you go in, and you set the time to 20 years from now. What will you see yourself doing? Be as precise as possible in your imagination, and then come back to the present time. Now, get up and start doing whatever it is that you want to do. Wear that bikini, climb that mountain, get out of that bad relationship, tell your boss you quit! Do not let fear limit your life. We only have one life, and there is no time machine. While you are still living, breathing, and being blessed each day with your health - be grateful for what you have, get rid of all your fears, crush all the walls of limitation, and put your dreams in the front seat again. Take Eleanor Roosevelt's advice: *"Do one thing every day that scares you."* Be courageous! Be fearless!

What Would You Do If You Weren't Afraid?

My answer is, *"I CAN DO EVERYTHING!"* It is so simple, yet so powerful! Can you see how much you can do if you do not have any fear? You can do everything! There are no limits!

Thinking back, I am glad for all the challenges in my life. I needed those to grow my belief and to know my purpose. Now, along the way, when fears creep back in, I know they are not real. I know yours aren't real either. I am not afraid of what success may bring anymore. I am stepping onto that playground. Let's run around the playground like crazy together.

Chapter 15

You Will Find Your Way

by Angelia Mantis

"Sometimes good things fall apart so better things can fall together."
~ Marilyn Monroe

Angelia Mantis

Angelia Mantis was born and raised in Montreal, Quebec, Canada and is a successful fashion entrepreneur. Her fascination with art and fashion began at a young age, as she has always had a broad and creative imagination. Creative design and laughter were, and still are, her form of therapy. She has a great appreciation for detail, as well as fine dining. Angelia is someone who sees opportunities and possibilities in life. Persistence is her strongest trait, and she has never been afraid of hard work.

Angelia is a self-taught, multi-business owner. Throughout her career, she focused on surrounding herself with ambitious and positive energy. Angelia is the designer and co-owner of Juliette Et Prince, her children's clothing line that she was inspired to create in late 2014. This year, she launched her latest business venture; a wedding garter line called Garterbox.

www.garterbox.com | Info@garterbox.com
ig: @Garterbox | fb: GARTERBOX

www.julietteetprince.com | info@julietteetprince.com
ig: @Julietteetprince | fb: julietteetprince

Growing up in a dysfunctional home, it was very hard for me to concentrate in school. I was immensely distracted by my private home life; I never put too much energy into my studies. My childhood forced me to grow up a lot faster than most girls my age. When I was eleven, I asked my mother if we could leave my father, and go live at my grandparents' house. She looked at me for a second; she didn't say no, she just asked me what my siblings would think. I could see it in her eyes that she secretly wanted out of her marriage, but never had the courage to do so. She never wanted to make the decision of having to take her children from their father. For the longest time, I was frustrated with my father for not seeing what a beautiful woman my mother is, and for leaving her at home most nights because gambling was a priority in his eyes when instead, it should have been his family. Over the years, I've made peace with this. I love my father very much. Being so young, I did not understand his choices back then. But nobody is perfect, I too, have made mistakes. I am very grateful for how my life turned out. I have been married seven years now, to the most amazing and supportive husband. Ladies, please don't ever settle for less! Your husbands should treat you like a queen, and if their mothers or any other parental figure has raised them properly, you will most likely get just that! Mothers, how beautiful are they? I have the most beautiful mother, but growing up I used to think my mother was weak. As harsh as that might sound, they still were my thoughts. However, as I grow older, I realize how strong she really was, and is today. Maybe as the years go by, I realize how much I mirror her. Her kind heart, her creative mind, she is always trying to make everyone happy and puts everyone else before herself. It is probably why we bicker so much, because we are so much alike.

Six years ago, I was working as an early childhood educator, and I decided that it was time to start my own family. Unfortunately, there was another plan for me; I miscarried. Twenty-five at the time, I remember living the most painful experience physically. I remember leaving the hospital feeling completely numb. I didn't cry that day, but boy did I feel empty. I'd compare my experience to the first time I was ever really heartbroken! What a shitty feeling, and as much as it hurt to experience all of it, it was a fact of life and would eventually guide me to the path I was destined to be on.

A month after miscarrying, I told my boss I was going to return to work. As months went by, I had started to feel extremely tired and started putting on extra weight - on top of the added stress-weight I had put on while planning my wedding years back. *Dear fat, fuck off.* Why does sugar exist right?

Maybe I Was Missing Something Else

Time went on in my career and marriage, but I never had the chance to heal, so I decided to see a therapist. I was shortly diagnosed with major depression disorder, which later turned into unbearable anxiety.

Depression was one of the lowest points in my life, and because of it, I had developed a whole other level of anxiety. I would question myself about everything. I had become fearful of things I was never fearful of prior in life. Being as anxious as I was, I always felt the need to tell people I was overweight because I miscarried; to justify why I was so heavy. That's how uncomfortable I felt in my own skin! *Why did I even have to explain myself?* As I grew older, I realized that I was trying to protect myself from all the thoughts I assumed everyone was thinking. When realistically, these thoughts were, in fact, my own perception of myself, which became my reality, and I thought this to be true.

For six months, getting out of bed was the hardest thing for me. I would sleep the days away, and it wasn't until months later in one of my behavioral therapy sessions, that my life would start to change. "Angie, what do you like to do?" asked Mrs. Therapist, "Pick a hobby and wake up to it every morning." So, I started to make hair accessories, and that is when my first business was born. I embraced my creative side. It was the only thing that kept me going, and got me out of bed in the morning. A few weeks later, I decided I would take my accessories and sell them around the city. I started to believe that the universe had bigger plans for me, and I knew it was up to me to make it all happen. I knew exactly who I wanted to start that venture with. I contacted the top-of-the-top department store! I decided to take a chance, *What is the worst that can happen? Would they say no? If I don't at least ask, it is still a no, so what's the harm in trying?* I got in contact with the buyer for accessories, and I asked her if she would be interested in seeing our collection in their department store. She replied kindly and said, "Unfortunately we are not looking to take on any more vendors." I was quick to reply persistently, "I am new to the industry. I can learn a lot from just a meeting with you, can you please meet with me, and if you are still not interested at least I've gotten an experience out of it!" She agreed, I assume she couldn't turn down my ambition! The day came, we met, and she absolutely loved everything and decided to take my collection and have it on consignment. She had given me the green light, which eventually opened many doors from there. I felt such excitement that day; I was so happy, I felt accomplished, I felt purpose, and I felt seen.

If You Want Something To Change, Start With You

I am not here to preach to you about the outcome, because it could have gone either way. I am here to tell you that even if that meeting had not gone as planned, I want you to trust that the next opportunity or the one after that will! I want you to take every situation as a learning experience, and it will help you grow along the way. Don't forget to challenge yourself, and more importantly envision yourself at your destination. You should be your biggest cheerleader, because if you don't believe in what you are working hard towards, why would anyone else? Do not be the only person getting in your own way of achieving great things.

My anxiety had taught me that when I allowed it to rule me, it was going to control my everyday life, and stop me from achieving my full potential. There were so many setbacks, until I realized I was so much stronger than "it." I wanted to start living again, and staying in my comfort zone was getting in the way of living such a beautiful hand I've been dealt. I can just scream out loud how blessed I am! We all are; we are alive, and that on its own is a gift!

I know sometimes it is hard to see the bright side of things. We all get caught up in our own gray thoughts; we would be lying if we said we didn't. But if you're reading this, I just want to let you know it is all going to be okay. Don't be so hard on yourself. Imagine obsessing about the things you love about yourself instead of burying your mind with self-doubt. Can't you see you would be unstoppable?

Dear reader, start living a fulfilled life, as you already are fulfilled with so much beauty. I promise the dream will come; with hard work and persistence, but most of all *self-belief* is where you will find what you are looking for.

The Doors Will Open If You Are Bold Enough To Knock

Putting my joy first is how I will live the most fulfilled life possible is what my life coach @whatconnects_us has taught me! Hearing those words really resonated with me, because looking back I never really did that. I was never first on my priority list; everyone else was, and that had to stop!

I am now living my life with purpose, and passion. I am the designer and co-owner of my children's clothing line Juliette Et Prince, and owner of my newest venture, GARTERBOX. I would like to leave you all with a little advice; be persistent, and believe in what you are selling. I have never been afraid of someone saying no, and neither should you. If you are afraid, then you are missing out on so many opportunities, and short changing yourself from the beautiful and prosperous life you are meant to live.

Along the way, you might get discouraged or distracted by others, and feel like there is no point in pursuing your passion. But just remember, self-doubt kills more dreams than failure ever will. You got this!

Chapter 16

The Power of Action

by Kelly Rolfe

"Strength doesn't come from what you can do. It comes from overcoming the things you once thought you couldn't." ~ Unknown

Kelly Rolfe

Kelly is a passionate woman with an intense desire to empower other women to be in complete love with themselves, and their lives. This is Kelly's second published project with Golden Brick Road Publishing House. She has also been featured as an author in *Dear Stress, I'm Breaking Up With You*. The Dear Series has been a beautiful outlet for Kelly to share her story as well as reach a broader audience of women on their path to success.

Through Kelly's personal journey of self-love, she found a passion for helping other women on their journey of health, happiness, and self-acceptance. This passion led her to become a health and fitness coach, life coach, author, and self-love warrior. Through these opportunities, Kelly has helped transform countless women's lives. She has not only supported their fitness journey but become a leader in finding self-love, self-worth, self-acceptance and internal happiness. Kelly believes that to love one's self truly, one must accept who they are while working towards who they want to be.

As Kelly continues to fulfill her dreams of success, entrepreneurship, and happiness, she can't help but feel like this will be a never-ending task. For every goal she achieves, she excitedly sets 10 more. This life has become a beautiful adventure for Kelly, and she is overjoyed that she was strong enough to chase her dreams. Join Kelly on this beautiful journey to bring out the strong, beautiful, capable, successful woman she knows is inside of you.

ig: mama_gets_fit_and_fab | fb: kelly.l.rolfe

I used to be the queen of limitations; I put them on myself all the time without even realizing it. I can't even tell you how many opportunities I've let pass me by because of my words, and / or actions. My actions and my hesitations about my self-worth were holding me back from living a life I loved. It took a lot of reflection, and a lot of self-awareness to realize that my limitations were all self-inflicted. The limits I was placing on myself turned out to be fear. My fears had taken complete control over my life both professionally, and personally. I was going through life just scraping by doing only what was required of me. I did not feel fulfilled. I did not feel passion. I could not see a happy future. It wasn't until I realized just how unhappy I was that I decided to build a life that I was passionate about. A life where work felt like joy. A life where I was limitless in my happiness, and my success. A life where fear became motivation and perceived limitations became a thing of the past. When I realized that fear had taken over my actions and placed limits on my life, I knew it was time to take action. To reclaim my life. And that is exactly what I did.

We have all heard the saying, *"It's not what you say, it's what you do,"* but in the world of limitations, it is both what you say and what you do (or don't do) that holds you back. Our actions and words have the power to launch us into endless possibilities, but they also have the power to limit every opportunity. Every time we say and / or do something, we are sending subconscious messages into the world. For example, when you arrive early to a meeting, you are setting the tone that you are punctual, invested, and prepared. These are obvious qualities that people want in a business partner or potential employee. On the flip side, when you arrive late to a meeting, you are setting the tone that the meeting is not important to you. Regardless of whether there was a legitimate reason, the person whom you've made wait could potentially perceive your tardiness as disrespectful, or that the purpose of the meeting was not important to you. The same goes with our verbal messaging; how many times have we said, "Oh maybe…" when we, in fact, meant no, when presented with a possible opportunity. Sometimes, we react that way because we were taken aback by the offer, or we are truly unsure of whether it is something of interest; the reasons don't really matter, what matters are the words that come out of our mouth. When we are not clear and concise with our words and actions, we are sending messages that we are not confident, and therefore inadvertently placing limitations on ourselves. When I think of how many limitations I could have put on myself while pursuing my dreams, the list would've been endless. As a single mother who was always working to make ends meet, I could have found a million reasons not to pursue my dreams. I don't have time, I don't have the money, and I need to have financial stability. All those things were true at the beginning of my entrepreneurial journey, but I made a conscious choice not to use those things as excuses to hold myself back, I had already done that for far too many years. I did not allow my perceived limitations to be anything but obstacles to overcome. I didn't have much time, so I made time. I started getting up earlier and stopped watching television in the evening. I didn't have much money to invest, so I did my research and invested what little money I had into things I was passionate about, that had the most lucrative opportunities. I did need financial stability, so I continued working at my full-time job while building my dreams outside of those 8 hours a day.

"The only limits in life are the ones you make."- Kristi Kremers

This quote couldn't be more true! I think it's important to clarify that I'm not talking about the big and blatant limitations we place on ourselves; I'm talking about the little ones we create for ourselves daily. We probably don't even realize we are limiting ourselves in those moments, but we are. This is true in all aspects of our lives. Let's take starting a health and fitness journey for example. You want to lose weight and live a healthy lifestyle, but how many limiting actions do we create as obstacles? We make excuses such as the added costs of buying healthy food, the time it takes to work out, and the fear surrounding starting something new. The truth is many of us will give up on the journey before it even begins. However, if you make a commitment to the journey you will realize that healthy food is no more expensive, you will become confident with your workouts the more you do them, you have an opportunity to meet like-minded people, and you will be filled with more energy, proper nutrition, and better sleep. The perceived obstacles are not fact; they are the mind using our fears to trick us into believing that we aren't capable. If you refuse to limit yourself, you will truly be unstoppable! You will realize that you can achieve anything you want. However, too often we create obstacles and limit ourselves beyond belief. Another example of how we might limit ourselves is through bad habits / addictions. Smoking, drinking, eating unhealthy, not getting enough sleep, serial dating, job hopping, etc. The list is endless, and the result is almost never positive. Our bad habits may seem personal and not relevant to our goals, but that is not the case. The things we do affect how the world sees us. It may seem unfair that we are judged by the choices we make in our personal time, however the way we present ourselves to the world has its consequences. How you present yourself to the world inevitably has a direct correlation with the types of people you attract. If you are pursuing a health and fitness journey, but you smoke and drink alcohol every weekend, it is unlikely that you will surround yourself with other people pursuing a healthy lifestyle, and therefore will limit yourself on your own journey.

One last example is a more detailed discussion about time management. Prioritization and time management are vital skills that all of us should possess. Don't get me wrong; I understand that we all have a million things to do every day, and so this may seem like a daunting task; however, once you master the skill of time management, all those things become possible to tackle. Prioritization is something that often bites me in the ass; I used to finish my preferred items first, but this just allowed me to continue to procrastinate my least favorite to-do items. But, I have found that when I do my least favorite things first, I feel more accomplished. This is because I have completed the necessary things off my list, not just the things that are easy or that I enjoy doing. The truth is I would do the enjoyable items anyways, so the completion of the not-so-great items make me feel accountable to my goals, and I end up completing more tasks. I live through lists; I make one every morning of all the things I absolutely need to get done that day. When I can see what needs to be done, I can then prioritize my list, and manage my time effectively. How do I know what should be done first? I look at my weekly goals, and I determine which goals are going to produce the most success in relation to my monthly goals. From there, I move down the list of "must do's" to complete all the goals I have developed. In the past, I was a master procrastinator and then spent my life scrambling to get things done. This increased my anxiety and left me in a constant state of panic. It was unhealthy, and it limited me in so many ways. I was not attracting stable and successful people in my life, I was not reflecting the kind of person I was (or was striving to be), and I certainly wasn't accomplishing my goals. So how do you break down limitations and build you own empire? A combination of things can help you to reach your ultimate potential.

"Many people are passionate, but because of their limiting beliefs about who they are and what they can do, they never take actions that could make their dream a reality." ~ Tony Robbins

Tips and tricks to break down limits:

Exude confidence! This is crucial when on your way to success. When we are just beginning our journey, it is natural not to feel confident in a world of unknowns. However, it is so important to present yourself in a manner that shows people that you believe in your success, goals, dreams, and plans. When we present ourselves as unsure, uncomfortable, or uncertain, it speaks volumes to potential business partners / employers. When you exude confidence, you are a force to be reckoned with. This will assist you in attracting like-minded people into your life, and assist you in reaching your goals.

Create a plan and set goals! Developing a plan of action will help you stay focused and committed to your goals. Building a plan needs to be clear and concise. Just writing down your goals can be helpful, but they serve more as affirmations than plans. When I first began my journey, I developed a detailed plan, and it was so incredibly helpful. My plan included timelines, goals, and methods on how I was going to reach those goals. Having it written out, and posted on my desk helped to keep me focused and assisted in turning my plan into my reality. It is so important to set goals for yourself. However, it is really important that we are setting attainable goals; otherwise, we tend to lose hope and motivation. I set weekly, monthly and quarterly goals for myself, and I find this to be very helpful. Setting clear, time sensitive, and attainable goals that pertain to your plan will continuously keep you feeling accomplished, confident, and quite honestly, like a successful bad ass!

Manage your time like a pro! I talked a bit earlier about being a procrastinator extraordinaire in my past life, and let me tell you, this did NOT serve me well. I somehow always managed to get things done, but I was not producing work that I could be proud of. My heart and my passion were not being shown in my work / product because I was not giving myself the time to produce something that was true to me and my vision. So, with that being said, time management is going to become your very best friend on your journey to breaking down limits and leading a life of success. I live in a world of to-do lists, and this works very well for me. Every Sunday, I make a weekly task list for the upcoming week. And then every morning, I make a list of things that need to get accomplished that day. Once my list is complete, I will often task things by the hour to ensure that I am keeping myself accountable within my working hours.

Prioritize in style! Now that you have time management down, it is important to prioritize that never-ending to-do list! Prioritization is key to breaking down limits and achieving success. Prioritizing deadlines, meetings, and tasks are vital to being productive and achieving your dreams. As previously mentioned, I always do my least favorite tasks first. We all have things that we *have to do* that we don't particularly enjoy, and these are usually the things that get pushed to the bottom of the list, and somehow never seem to get done until the very last possible moment. I challenge you to change that! I challenge you to do these things first and here's why: when we stop procrastinating, we end up accomplishing more than we ever thought we could.

Follow through! Now let's tie it all together. We've talked about prioritizing, time management, setting goals, planning and being confident. All these tips can be incredibly helpful, but only if we act on it, stop limiting ourselves, and follow through! This chapter is about what we say and do (or don't say and don't do) that limits us on our journey to success. Following through will not only help you to complete tasks, meet deadlines, and reach goals, but it will assist you in being confident!

I completely understand that all these tips and tricks may seem daunting, and overwhelming. However, if you are on a journey of change and success, these things are necessary!

"Believe that there are no limitations, no barriers to your success – you will be empowered, and you will achieve." ~ Ursula Burns

Limitations can feel very real and debilitating if you aren't equipped with the tools and the motivation to push through them. However, limitations only have the power to hold you back from your goals, if you allow them. I promise you that every successful person that you admire has overcome perceived limitations. They have done just what you are doing now; researched, found strategies that work for them, acted upon those strategies, and persevered! Just like any other obstacle, you are capable of pushing through and overcoming limits to reach your dreams. You are strong, you are motivated, and you can get those limits out of your way! By following the tips and tricks in this chapter and all the others in this book, I am confident that you will be limitless! For more motivation, tips, tricks on being limitless, loving yourself and achieving your goals email me at kelly.rolfe@gmail.com.

Chapter 17

Limits Are A Decision, It Is Your Choice

by Ky-Lee Hanson

"If you are constantly trying to satisfy your fulfillment through the choices and direction of other people, you will have little management over your own perception." ~ Ky-Lee Hanson

Ky-Lee Hanson

Bosswoman | Visionary | Creator of opportunity & motivation

Ky-Lee Hanson is the kind of individual who was glad to turn 30. She is an old soul who gets the big picture. She is built on hope, and believes in equality. She is optimistic, but understands things for what they really are. Ky-Lee enjoys people. She finds them fascinating. Her studies in sociology, human behavior, stress management, nutrition and health sciences has led her to have a deep understanding of people. Being someone who can spot potential, one of the hardest things she ever had to learn was, "You can't help someone who doesn't want to help themselves."

Growing up, she had a hard time understanding why people couldn't seem to live the lives they dreamed of. Often thinking she must be the main character in a world similar to The Truman Show, because nothing seemed to make sense; she always saw things differently, and found it hard to relate to people. This ended up sending her into a downward spiral in her twenties, when she felt she had no choice but to settle. She felt suppressed, limited, and angry. Ky-Lee has the ability to hyper focus and learn things quickly. She has a power-mind and found the true strength of life through a serious health battle in her late twenties. Ky-Lee took control and over the years, mastered how to get her power back. She discovered the best way to "relate" to people is not to, instead simply listen to understand their world for the uniqueness that it is.

Ky-Lee is a 2x best selling author, and a successful entrepreneur. She thrives on creating opportunities to help people along their journey. Her success came by developing the taboo art of collaborative business. Ky-Lee has an open-door policy she learnt from her mom, a listening ear, and an opportunity to lock arms and take you down your Golden Brick Road.

www.goldenbrickroad.pub
ig: kylee.hanson.bosswoman | fb: kylee.hanson

Entrepreneurial-minded people simply see obstacles as opportunities, and not only in business, but as a way of life. Our authors see progress as the only way to live. Taking strategic chances, being excited about risk, believing in themselves, and finding the opportunity behind every obstacle. Could it be that our limit *is* our opportunity? Could our limit be our answer to a breakthrough? Could our limit be there to develop our ultimate strength? Shift the definition of limit; as we all have. See your limits as the fuel you need, in order to grow. Do not be scared or ashamed to define areas in which you can develop.

I often feel that I am not as attentive as I would like to be in my roles as a sister, daughter, friend or girlfriend, but – there is a but, I am on a mission to better us all. In retrospect, it is the opposite; I am very attentive to everyone's needs, and I am doing my part to correct the pain in the world by leading by example and dedicating my life to creating positive change. My personal sacrifice is the greatest gift I can give. This chapter will guide us to accept and honor the decision-making process. A limit is nothing but a decision, something accepted as a way of life. It is our choice to see something as a sacrifice or an opportunity. *In order to achieve, I must do this and must stop doing that.* This book has provided dozens of examples where women have made a choice to take the lead in their life, to create their path and persevere; as a result, they became stronger and arrived at the places they wanted to be. Almost always, getting past or preventing limitations means some sort of sacrifice. Sacrifice is not always bad; sometimes it is freeing! Sometimes it is temporary, and sometimes it takes an adjustment.

Are You Maximizing Your Life?

The most crippling limitations are the ones we do not realize we have. We have yet to make a conscious decision if we are going to let it have control over us or not. We can be oblivious to controlling factors. Things, people, routine, habits, desires, beliefs, and addictions can consume us. What I see in many of my prospects, clients, friends, family and within society (I have also been here many times, and in some ways I still am) is a norm of being unaware of limits and blocking factors. Granted, we never know everything going on in another person's world, what "I see" sometimes is simply just that. However, in my line of work, people confide in me; I read their raw stories, I help them dig deeper, and I share with them what I perceive. Often, we need an outside perspective to show us what is right in front of our eyes - and yes - often it is a big giant brick wall, but the right discussion can crush down that wall and turn it into a golden brick road. *See what I did there...* We have made it quite clear that the words and actions of others can limit us; however, we also know that the right conversation can provide abundance.

In this book, we talked about self-limitations, as well as external and social restrictions which hinder us from success and happiness with our career, body image, environments, lifestyle and relationships. It *all* comes back around to self-awareness, furthering education, trying new things, gaining self-esteem, and building confidence. It is becoming more common to strive towards consciousness; the state of being awake, and aware of one's surroundings. A way to look at it is, think before you speak, think before you act, and think before you *interact*. It also means to respect and acknowledge the world around you, and to say, do, and be in the present moment; be aware of the effect you have on the world, and the effects it has on you.

We each have our own outlook and unique experience of the world; no two people have the exact same surroundings, sight, thoughts or interactions, causing each life to be on its own path towards achieving its individual wants and needs. I reference this as *our world*, meaning in a sense of ownership. It is our very own. We visit each other's worlds and pick up tidbits of information, as well as experiences both positive, and negative. It is our choice how we let this influence us. We can stay awhile and live in someone else's world, learning much from them and adding pieces of them to our own world. We can absorb both positive and negative; the difference is deciding if you learn from the negative or accept it in as a way of life. We can allow the negative in, as long as we decide it cannot stay. Are we going to let a painful situation such as broken trust or inequality make us an angry person, or will we be strong and let it be a reminder of why we personally only portray good into society? This is an example of taking an experience that could become a limit, but instead finding the opportunity within it. It is important to experience the bad to appreciate the good; to help us grow in different ways. What it comes down to is, we influence the world in which we live. We have to look at ourselves as our own day to day creator. What are you going to make happen today? If the people around you, the environment, the job, etc. do not cater to it, find other worlds to step into, and see how they live. Adopt some new customs and new habits. Positive people are always willing to help others. Be careful though, negativity sometimes wears a welcoming-mask; negative people love company, and will latch on and try to make you fit into their world. They will encourage you to act toxic, possibly to be unhealthy, miss work, complain, make fun of others, and put off your dreams.

"Great minds discuss ideas; average minds discuss events; small minds discuss people." ~ Lady Eleanor Roosevelt

Much of our time is spent working at tasks in our external world. Some people rarely spend time on their personal development, nor condition with self-care such as deep thought, positive thinking, reading, meditation, a pampering bath, or watching an inspiring movie, or guilty-pleasure TV show (Nashville and teen dramas over here!). Do you really know what gives you pleasure without the involvement of anyone else? It may be swimming, or walking, or shopping. However, it cannot be swimming for fitness based on looking a certain way, it cannot be walking to work while checking emails, and it cannot be shopping for your kids or bring on guilt that you spent money on shoes for yourself - *shoes are always approved!* It has to be for your own peace. I spent the last four years of my life, living for ME. It was lonely to adjust to; I had to learn how to be strict to my wants, needs, and beliefs, and yet be consciously open minded. I quickly found that a lot of people around me either did not understand me, did not want to grow with me or did not have my best interests at heart. I was constantly thrown obstacles that limited me such as judgment from others and self judgment. Growth is not easy, self-care looks selfish. You are going to need to be open minded, and you may find yourself exploring things that other people are yet to understand; new diets, new medicinals, new fashion styles, new spending habits, holistic practices, hiring a maid or extra help, reiki, meditation, and travel. Maybe you will decide to throw your tv away, or delete Facebook. Maybe you will take up a sport. These may be drastic and temporary, but you cannot grow, nor make an informed decision until you experience something. If a person is not open to trying, without an educated reason as to why not, they are limiting themselves. I am not a self-care coach, but I can tell you, four years of personal development and self-care made me the powerhouse in business that I am today. You cannot have one without the other. The audiobook *Emotional Intelligence: What Makes a Leader?* by Daniel Goleman helped me to confirm my own growth. I encourage you to listen even if you feel you are not a leader - you do need to lead your own life. And for the areas of your self awareness that you are still working on; do not see it as a limit, do not compare yourself to others, instead see it as an opportunity to grow.

What Are Some Limits You May Not Realize You Have?

Concept Of Time - always late, over or under estimating timelines, or procrastination. Those are the effects but what is the cause? Could it be self sabotage? Lack of interest / wrong environment? Or maybe a lack of learning how to organize your time?

A Lacking Environment - feeling unstimulated, depressed, stuck. Developing negative habits - emotional eating, drinking, over binging on tv? Maybe you are in a routine that you have outgrown?

Un-organization - do you have a feeling of chaos in your life? Are you flustered, misplacing things, accidentally putting things off, missing messages and finding yourself saying, "Ah, I can't believe I forgot." Maybe you are lacking a system, some guidance, some training on how to allocate and delegate tasks.

Limited Knowledge or Experience - you may find yourself getting into arguments often, defending your beliefs or feeling self conscious about what you can achieve. Maybe there are new skills within you to develop, new interests to explore, a greater understanding of the human condition and the study of people.

176

Fear; Of The Unknown, Of Failure, Of Rejection - living a very controlled and cautious life. Living in routine but secretly wishing for more. An effect of fear is comparing yourselves to others, jealousy, expectations and anxiety. You may need to realize how unique you are, how capable humans are. Remember that people do not regret the chances they took, they regret the ones they didn't take.

Money Control - emotional spending. Do you shop to make yourself happy, to try and fill a void? Do you dress or furnish your home a certain way to be accepted by others? Shopaholics are typically looking to fill a space. I used to be one. Retail therapy made me feel good, made me feel "able" to take care of myself, made me feel new and happy in a fresh outfit, or with something new for my home or business. That feeling would fade. It was not the addressing the cause, only the effect. Maybe you cannot save money, or cannot seem to pay off your debt. It is quite common in our society, but maybe there is something causing your inability to be stable; you are used to chaos in your life and the relationship you have with money could be unstable.

In all cases, you need to identify the problem; the effects in your life. From there, identify the root cause. Seek help for the root cause, and change the effects. There is help out there for all causes. Make sure you talk to someone, read the book, and do the practices necessary not only to change the effect, but to get to the cause.

Can You Do It?

How many times do you run around the house or the office saying, *I can't find it*, only to realize, once you have a clearer mind, or you ask someone else, it was in front of you the entire time. If you approached the situation and said to yourself, "I am finding…" or simply focusing on it and nothing else, not listening to the chatter, *I'm late*, or *ah, why can't I find it*, you will probably find it much easier. You are not distracted or cluttered with worry or uncertainty, you just are, and it just is. Life goes on under less stress, and without limits. This sense of awareness can be used for more productive things of course.

"I think 99 times and find nothing. I stop thinking, swim in the silence, and the truth comes to me." ~ *Albert Einstein*

The same goes for when you tell yourself you can't achieve, such as starting a new career or business, losing weight and getting healthy, taking on a second job, or fitting in a hobby or something just for you into your week. *I don't know if I can find the time,* or *I wish I had that motivation,* or *I don't know what I am doing,* or *I am not very tech savvy.* If you approach situations with a CAN-DO attitude or simply a doing / it's happening attitude, trust me, it is much easier. You *are* capable of learning. It is hard *only* if you make it so with your own limitations. You can ask for help, you can google your question – *did you know that – sometimes I wonder...* I get asked the simplest questions sometimes. A person can literally Google anything and get answers. It is right in front of us. Following, is an example of where I need to take my own advice; *do as I say, not as I do...* Often, I will ask my spouse questions that I know he knows, or will be able to figure out quicker than I would on my own. I unconsciously choose to not stay up to the most current trends with technology, and it is extremely limiting in many aspects of my life. I don't update my cell phone, so it now runs slow. I don't update my laptop, so it runs slow. I overpack my schedule, and do not use the necessary technology and organizational things to make my life easier. I am the one creating this limit because I try to breeze past the things of no interest - however, they are vital to my success. It is important to realize we are not as skilled as others, and it is okay to not know everything, nor have the time to master it. My spouse knows everything about software and technology or if he doesn't, it is easier for him to understand a situation - quicker - than it is for me. However, when I ask him to do things for me, I am limiting myself to his understanding, and I am expecting a quick and easy answer usually throwing him off course of what he was doing, as my question is unrelated, and usually I deliver it in a hasty - right now - way. He tells me to Google things, I feel frustrated - *why can't you just tell me* - well guess what, he does tell me and the next day I need to ask again! I did not do it nor learn it for myself.

"Tell me and I forget, teach me and I may remember, involve me and I learn." ~ Benjamin Franklin

Do Not Compare Your Dream Life to Someone Else's Dream Life

Am I a realistic person? Um, in a traditional sense, no. *"Being realistic is the most commonly traveled road to mediocrity" ~ Will Smith.* I know that with a willing attitude there is way. That is real, so everything is realistic in that sense. I know what is capable of being done, but do I always give it a realistic timeline? No. But, do I get it done? Yes. Most people would look at my life and say it's not possible in that time frame. It's February and I've had a handful of big shifting discussions where people said one thing or another was not possible but I did it. I did ALL OF IT. When someone says something is unrealistic, they are basing it on their own limitations. Do not listen to them. If you are really contemplating something, there is a spark proving that it IS possible. Shoot me an email, let's talk it out. Your will is the way.

While we are on the topic of mediocrity, this word means to live or to be only of moderate quality, to be not very good... I came across an article called, *What if All I Want is a Mediocre Life?* The author Krista O'Reilly Davi-Digui states, "...Loud, haranguing voices lecturing me to hustle, to improve, build, strive, yearn, acquire, compete, and grasp for more. For bigger and better. Sacrifice sleep for productivity. Strive for excellence. Go big or go home. Have a huge impact in the world. Make your life count. But what if I just don't have it in me. What if all the striving for excellence leaves me sad, worn out, depleted? Drained of joy. Am I simply not enough?" and, "What if I never really amount to anything when I grow up - beyond mom and sister and wife?" and ends with, "What if I embrace my limitations and stop railing against them? Make peace with who I am and what I need and honor your right to do the same. Accept that all I want is a small, slow, simple life. A mediocre life. A beautiful, quiet, gentle life."[14] Whatever your goal is, whatever makes you

---

[14]Davi-Digui, K. O. (n.d) *What if All I Want is a Mediocre Life?* Retrieved from https://nosidebar.com/mediocre-life/

get up in the morning and excited to live that day - IS NOT medio-cre. There is a difference between having a life that gives you enough / everything versus settling / comparing. My life is more so the life she is choosing to see full of limitations and struggle to reach. How-ever, it does not take sacrificing sleep for productivity (quite the op-posite, if you do not sleep well, you will burn out and be very unsuc-cessful) and there is zero competition in my life. I choose to work collectively. The above story strives for a simpler life *but* I would not consider that "mediocre." I personally don't strive to live in a small town with kids but that does not make it wrong. It is a simple life to her, but would be a struggle for me. It would not be my ideal environment. This again comes down to the common theme of our book. You cannot compare your situation to anyone else. You cannot compare your dreams and desires to anyone else. As I mentioned before, we each have our own outlook and unique experience of the world, no two people have the exact same surroundings, sight, thoughts or interactions, causing each life to be on its own path towards achieving its individual wants and needs. For those that DO want to be super-achievers, "You have the same number of hours in the day as Beyoncé... 'super-achievers' have the same number of hours in the day as the rest of us, but somehow, they always seem to get more done. How do they do it?"[15] The 28-year career of Dr. Suzanne Gelb suggests: fully commit, avoid multi-tasking, ban 'friendly-interruptions' at all costs, hang with fellow super-achievers, and prevent emotions from building.

This does not have to be a struggle, you do not need to give up the things you love, or become someone you are not – you simply have to master what drives you. When you analyze your life based on cause and effect, it is quick to weed out what does not serve you. From there you can structure / design a routine and way of life that works for you.

I am always challenging myself and focus more on the details of what I need in place for the dream life to be reality. I have made a

---

[15]Suzanne Gelb, PHD, JD. (n.d). How Successful People Do More in 24 Hours Than the Rest of Us Do in a Week. Retrieved from https://www.themuse.com/advice/how-successful-people-do-more-in-24-hours-than-the-rest-of-us-do-in-a-week/?

conscious decision to grow, to "work hard," and get what I want in life. There is no special skill, I am not a genius, I did not come from money, I do not even have a degree. I am well educated - studying many things, many courses, learning from many, and applying new things daily. I read, I write, I ask questions and I listen. All day, every day. As I wrote in my last book, give yourself just one thing – an inquisitive mind. The answers are out there. Be a sponge for knowledge. We are creatures of habit, and once you start doing this, you will come to love it. You will see the changes in your life, you will begin to enjoy your own mind and your own company - there is nothing greater, I promise you that.

I Will Not Put Effort Into *Anything* If There Is No Risk

What I mean is, it's wasteful to consider doing something that is easy, routine, or "safe" because it will never demand effort from me which makes it - frivolous. This was an extremely pivotal moment for me when I realized this. I ask myself now, "Is this frivolous or productive?" Everything I do, must serve my future. Sometimes that looks like relaxing, laughing and spending way too much money out on a nice dinner. This is self-cafe but is an indirect part of productivity. If it is going out simply because I am bored, or with people that provide no structured or stimulating conversation - that is frivolous. If there is a project I am offered that has no challenge to it - it is frivolous / waste of my time. My projects need to be on brand and encourage me to grow, master a skill and allow for me to teach others. Within challenging productivity is where you find your passion. Passion is not routine, passion does not know repetition. Passion is a life force.

It's during the hardest times that we endure the biggest transformations. Life is a series of challenges. We decide if they stop us, or strengthen us. We can run away from challenges but they are still there, now a black cloud or an overgrown golden brick road, we simply chose to not take the chance to come out from under the clouds or clear the path. Worthwhile things take time to cultivate. Challenges always look risky. We don't know how they are going to play out. Why do some people run from challenges and risks, and others seem like they are always out on a limb, standing on 1 foot, jugging then jumping? I'm a jumper, so let's talk about that. I heard a study once, I cannot remember where but it has always stuck with me, it said people who take risks vs people who do not take risks both have an equal chance of failure. Ok, so I thought, why not? There is the chance of financial failure, relationship failure, and failure every-which-way anyways; I have the same odds either way, so why not learn and grow, even if something doesn't work out? There is always a positive to trying something. Life can be "safe" or it can be full of stories!

"Entrepreneurs eat fear and failure for breakfast!" ~ *Ky-Lee Hanson*

Business people say, your failures are your biggest successes. I full heartedly know this to be true. I'm optimistic, and never see anything as a failure, but always as a learning experience, a stepping stone. It comes down to what success is to you. Is it money or something more? True entrepreneurs are invested in becoming the best version of themselves. They know things are going to be challenging. It's always too early to quit. What business and life is about, is growing. We need to stop being in a hurry to the end, and focus on becoming strong enough for what is coming.

Please never decide against something you want because you feel it isn't the right time. Never feel like you only get one shot, trust me, you get lots of opportunities. You can always try again, reinvent yourself and start over - only wiser. Do not wait "for the perfect moment," and do not be anxious about failure. Everything you do that is a little bit scary, gets you closer to being your ultimate self. If you keep waiting, and keep saying no to opportunities because it doesn't look 100% right or something *could* go wrong, if you keep saying no - I feel you may never get there.

"Change your story, change your life. Divorce the story of limitation, and marry the story of the truth and everything changes." ~ *Tony Robbins*

No person is born into their ultimate greatness. It is something that is cultivated, torn at, redeveloped and nurtured. I feel that society is weak because many of us never learn how to ask for help. We choose to not accept imperfection for the gift it truly is.

To be a true life designer or entrepreneur, it is never about "having enough". It is a different way of thinking. What *is* "enough" is the - creating. The hustle is not a limit, it is the opportunity. It *is* the desire. It *is* the passion. It is the never-ending "end-zone". It is the place we want to be. A dreamer is only satisfied when they *are dreaming*, when they are creating and working through limitations. It is 100% about how you approach situations. Is your life moving and developing or is it standing still? This is not defined by how much money you have, how many achievements, how many fans or followers or how many possessions are in your life. It is about a sense of movement and feeling fulfilled within that movement. This is called momentum. Momentum IS the biggest achievement for a dreamer and luckily we can choose to always stay and live within this zone. In turn, always feeling fulfilled. It is not about where you came from and where you are going but about how you are moving through life.

Acknowledgments

Thank you to the amazing team that has come together through the development of this book. Thank you to Tania J Moraes-Vaz, Ben Coles, Jessica Deaken, Natalie Barratt, Tara Mixon and all my limitless contributing authors. This book has been a major player in our career growth as a publishing house and book series. Seriously, obstacles constantly showed up and we kept crushing them! Everything wrong - went wrong - but we moved past it all; and are hella strong now and experienced because of it. Our limits were our opportunities to BE better. ~ Ky-Lee Hanson

Thank you to my wonderful family. You make my heart smile every day. ~ Jewell Siebert

I thank God for his graces and unconditional love. I thank my husband Jon, and children - Jessica, Jack, and Paige for lighting up my life. ~ Cindi Melkerson

Thank you to my husband, Jordan, who has inspired me to be fearless. ~ Emily Marie Gruzinski

This book will not be possible without the support of all the rockstars in my family. Thank you Francesco, Carina, Gaspare, Susanti, and Susiana, I love you all! ~ Rusiana T Mannarino

This chapter is for the amazing women in my life including my mom, aunts, cousins, friends, and my Grammas. ~ Shelbi De Silva

I thank my rock, my husband, Brad, and our gorgeous boys. Also, thank you to all the people who suggested against following my dreams, for making me push harder to achieve them. ~ Sabrina Greer

I'm so grateful for the queens, kings, and the prince in my life who stood with me through my 3B's. ~ Vickee Love

So much love and gratitude to my spiritual mentors and teachers; in every single disguise ~ Jennifer Jayde

This is just the beginning of our beautiful life. Cheers to unraveling the many more wonderful layers of our future. I love you Andrew!
~ Angelia Mantis

I give thanks to my TRIBE. You know who you are; strong, independent beauties. Thank you to my supportive husband, Scott.
~ Elaine McMillan

Thank you to my daughter for being an inspiration in my life as I continue to venture out in my career. ~ Deirdre Slattery

Thank you to my parents for their constant support, and to my amazing husband for his love, and unending belief in me! ~ Lisa Gartly

Thank you to all the amazing, strong, and fearless women in my life. Your support means everything. ~ Kelly Rolfe

In loving memory of my Granny Leitch. Who always defied the limits. ~ Jess Arbour

Thank you to my amazing fiancé, Simon, for his unwavering encouragement, and support. ~ Shabira Wahab

To my husband Karim, and our beautiful daughter Zelda Skye, you have taught me what unconditional love really means.
~ Katherine Debs

Find the rest of the Dear Women Guide Book Series at www.gbragency.com or from your favorite book retailer online.

Golden Brick Road
Publishing House

Locking arms and helping each other down their Golden Brick Road

At Golden Brick Road Publishing House, we lock arms with ambitious people and create success through a collaborative, supportive, and accountable environment. We are a boutique shop that caters to all stages of business around a book. We encourage women empowerment, and gender and cultural equality by publishing single author works from around the world, and creating in-house collaborative author projects for emerging and seasoned authors to join. Our authors have a safe space to grow and diversify themselves within the genres of poetry, health, sociology, women's studies, business, and personal development.

We help those who are natural born leaders, step out and shine! Even if they do not yet fully see it for themselves. We believe in empowering each individual who will then go and inspire an entire community. Our Director, Ky-Lee Hanson, calls this The Inspiration Trickle Effect.

If you want to be a public figure that is focused on helping people and providing value, but you do not want to embark on the journey alone, then we are the community for you.

To inquire about our collaborative writing opportunities or to bring your own idea into vision, reach out to us at www.goldenbrickroad.pub